To Dear Cole
with love and thanks for all those
wonderful weekends

BLOKES

Also by David Castronovo

Critic in Love: A Romantic Biography of Edmund Wilson (with Janet Groth)

*Beyond the Gray Flannel Suit: Books From the 1950s That
    Made American Culture*

Edmund Wilson: The Man in Letters (edited with Janet Groth)

Edmund Wilson Revisited

Richard Yates: An American Realist (with Steven Goldleaf)

From the Uncollected Edmund Wilson (edited with Janet Groth)

The American Gentleman

The English Gentleman

Thornton Wilder

Edmund Wilson

BLOKES

The Bad Boys of English Literature

David Castronovo

continuum

NEW YORK • LONDON

2009

The Continuum International Publishing Group Inc
80 Maiden Lane, New York, NY 10038

The Continuum International Publishing Group Ltd
The Tower Building, 11 York Road, London SE1 7NX

www.continuumbooks.com

ISBN 978-0-8264-2832-5

Library of Congress Cataloging-in-Publication Data
Castronovo, David.
Blokes : the bad boys of English literature / David Castronovo.
  p. cm.
  Includes bibliographical references and index.
  ISBN-13: 978-0-8264-2832-5 (hardcover : alk. paper)
  ISBN-10: 0-8264-2832-0 (hardcover : alk. paper)
1. English literature—20th century—History and criticism.
2. Literature and society—Great Britain—History—20th century.
3. Authors, English—20th century—Political and social views.
4. Male authors, English—Attitudes. 5. Social classes in literature.
6. Reality in literature. 7. Social problems in literature. 8. Radicalism in
literature. I. Title. II. Title: Bad boys of English literature.

PR478.S64C37 2009
820.9'9286709045—dc22   2008045811

Typeset by Newgen Imaging Systems Pvt Ltd, Chennai, India
Printed in the United States of America

For Val and Janet, Alan and Olivia

Contents

1

THE BLOKE: A VERY SHORT LITERARY HISTORY

Aggression, self-assertion, the pursuit of pleasure, the generating of mischief and transgressive humor, the flight from traditional disciplines and codes, the contempt for institutions, the boredom with routine, the struggle to live vitally: these are the marks of a social type and a recurring figure in English literature and life. The bloke is a male who believes in his own spirit and is willing to do almost anything to see that its spark doesn't die. Difficult, contrarian, insulting, most often a drinker and a teller-off of his contemporaries, he is a type who insists on himself and will follow no conventional path in his pursuit of more life, more pleasure, and more honesty. The age old idea of the gentleman is at war with the bloke: it ritualizes aggression and pleasure. It has turned aggression into family pride and obsession with ancestry, into the code of the duel from the middle ages through the nineteenth century, into the defensive etiquette and fine manners found in courtesy books from the Renaissance though the twentieth century, and lately into every kind of exclusivity and snobbery based on money and achievement. Gentlemen have also ritualized their pleasures—connoisseurship, clubs, beautiful domestic and academic surroundings, fashionable places.

But blokes improvise, trust their instincts and take life as it comes, having their fights and their fun without elaborate rules and conventions. The bloke, like the gentleman, has traveled a long road in English culture—from Chaucer's randy students in *The Miller's Tale* and *The Reeve's Tale*, to Falstaff, to eighteenth century picaros, to nineteenth century fictional characters like Dickens's Sam Weller and real-life authors such as William Hazlitt, to twentieth century protesters against the genteel including D. H. Lawrence and George Orwell, and to the leaders of the bloke revolt at mid-century, Kingsley Amis, Philip Larkin, and John Osborne. That road leads to figures of our own time such as Nick Hornby, A. A. Gill, and Martin Amis. The bloke, like the gentleman, is not merely a man with a particular status: he is a collection of attitudes and behavior patterns, tending—it's true—to be found in the humbler regions of society; but he can be found higher up on the social ladder, particularly because of education and money. Blokes may go to Oxford and Cambridge, but Oxford and Cambridge don't go to the heart of what a bloke is: for that we need to investigate a number of writers, the characters they brought to life, and the various forms that blokish living assumed as it defied gentlemanly living.

The bloke emerged as an important figure in national culture during the 1940s, just as the gentleman was becoming an anachronism, a faded ideal, a damaged player in novels, poems, and drama. Graham Greene's seedy protagonists—run-down gents consumed by inner torment—signal the start. As far back as 1935 in his novel *England Made Me* Greene was cynical about his gentleman protagonist Anthony Farrant, a do-nothing public school boy who pretends to be an old Harrovian. His sister secured him a job with her industrialist lover's firm in Sweden. We watch the gentleman Farrant—with his pretenses and snobbery—fall afoul of the hard-edged businessman Krogh and wind up dead. Farrant has a sometime pal and watcher of the big man, an impecunious journalist named Minty; this fellow is another pathetic relic of the public school system. He thinks of himself as a spider under a toothbrush cup. In *Brighton Rock* there's a corrupt lawyer who wonders what his public school master would think of his activities as a gangster's counselor. And then in Greene's most successful period there are the main characters of *The End of the Affair* and *The Heart of the Matter*, both men of social standing who are in a sorry state. Out in Africa as a policeman, Scobie in *The Heart of the Matter* commits a dreadful sin resulting in a man's death; he takes his own life soon after. The protagonist of *The End of the Affair* has transgressed against the code of honor and decency, and would be happy to go on doing so if God would let him. His beloved Sarah, the wife of another man, prays for his salvation during the Blitz and promises God to end the affair. He lives— but in agony. Such fragile gents are falling apart in the name of metaphysical disturbances and moral problems that a disciplined gentleman could handle. Greene's gentlemen despair about everything from their own natures to God's forgiveness. They're not strong, and their author does nothing to glamorize them. On the other hand Evelyn Waugh believes in the gentlemen's values and in his strength, but knows the game is up. *Brideshead Revisited* overflows with nostalgia and sentiment for the aristocracy and gentry, pity and love for an order ruined by years of economic decline, by the ravages of two wars, and by the leveling of society after World War II. The fall is tragic rather than ironically gruesome in Greene's manner, but it is still a fall. Marchmain House in London has been torn down years ago; Brideshead is empty except for the troops that are billeted there. Among the recruits is one Hooper, an affable but clueless young fellow who has no idea what such a place could be for. Waugh mocks him—but what's the good? The Hoopers are the inheritors of the British nation. Blokes are on the march.

Clement Attlee's victory over Churchill for the prime ministership in the defining election of 1945—the ouster of the Duke of Marlborough's descendent by a solicitor's son—was symbolic of the nation's mood. The people wanted a different idea of a leading man (and solid practicalities in place of the valiant blood, sweat, and tears). The veteran of socialist meetings and scrappy campaigns against the privileged went mano-a-mano with the man of the cigars, the homburg, the almost Lancastrian eloquence. It turned out that labor reform, health care, and education were on Britishers' minds, not glory and the Empire. Britishers were not, like their American allies, feeling triumphant. As Malcolm Bradbury so brilliantly put it in *No, Not Bloomsbury*, "Though not a defeated nation, post-war Britain was a depleted nation, touched by the feelings of historical ruination that were running through battle worn, seedy, economically troubled and politically fearful Europe." Corelli Barnett's *The Lost Victory* is an account of why Britain went downhill in the late 1940s: too many illusions. On the left were ill-conceived ideas about social planning instead of industrial recovery, on the right hopelessly useless ideas about Empire and the value of Victorian-style elitist education. When Clement Attlee replaced Churchill, old ideals of national pride didn't have enough to say about jobs and housing; at the same time "The New Jerusalem" of a prosperous welfare state involved vague tomorrows, bureaucracy, rules, and more run-arounds for those who went out to work. Finally, according to Barnett, the long-term stagnation of the economy set in and with it a sense that Britain had lost an Empire and new possibilities as well. Caught between two dreamy worlds—the old pomp and circumstance of Churchill, the new welfare state policies of Attlee—the British male of this generation became restless and frustrated and numbers of writers stepped up to document his feelings. In *Casino Royale* (1953), Ian Fleming did his outrageous bit for the male spirit by fusing the bloke and the gentleman. James Bond was sexual and aggressive in the extreme, and yet he had the aura and traditional values and social graces of the Establishment. Kingsley Amis, that leader of the bloke revolution, even took a hand in writing a James Bond novel titled *Colonel Sun*; by all accounts a fairly mechanical treatment of foreign baddies vs. Bond, it shows Amis putting his aggression at the service of British spiritedness. But the main thread of our story is the British bloke acting out his nature against the backdrop of a fragile nation, one with diminished prospects, one that needed someone more everyday than Bond to brace it up. Doing one's bit was no longer very appealing; doing something glamorous seemed out of the question for many; getting one's own back was what was called for. The bloke's impolite style of assertion—vulgar language, rude sentiments, disregard for others' feelings, humorous disdain for the venerable and the traditional and the dignified, and undisguised selfishness—become the dominant form of being male. The years 1945–65 were the golden ones for bloke culture: a group of writers flourished who lived the life and set down versions of behavior that are an enduring part of English history. Some older writers applauded the vitality of the new man; but others like Somerset Maugham and Evelyn Waugh thought he was "scum." "No charity, kindliness, and generosity," according to Maugham, to be found in "the white-collar proletariat" with their love of getting the best for themselves and getting down to the pub. Yet most barometric readings indicated that something big was happening.

By 1956, the new culture of discontent and resentment was brought to a boil by the Suez Crisis. This botch in foreign affairs—involving an old order Prime Minister Anthony Eden who used force against Arab nationalists, a grave miscalculation about England's strength, and dreams of restored Empire dashed practically overnight—occurred in the same year as John Osborne's *Look Back in Anger*. The play shocked the nation culturally and secured new prestige for the English tradition of sharp social criticism at a time when it was most needed. Osborne offset Eden, as it were, by showing that it was time to drop the pretensions and illusions and become angry about a country in the spiritual and cultural doldrums. And there was to be no peace about British values, British hierarchies, British stuffiness, and nostalgia thereafter. A restless bloke and his play, as we shall see, were only part of the firestorm of criticism—and not the first on the field against the old order. Cambridge historian Peter Mandler in his study *The English National Character* has shown the What's-Wrong-With-Britain question turning into a sustained attack on the Establishment, a term that gathered bad connotations as the 1950s and 1960s rolled on. "They"—the amateurs and gentleman who ran the nation—had landed "us" in a fine mess. In a famous volume of 1957 called *Declaration*, edited by young Tom Maschler (later to establish the Booker Prize), Osborne joined other malcontents by contributing his broadside "And They Call It Cricket": "I can't go on laughing at the idiocies of the people who rule our lives." Peter Mandler draws attention to a passage the aggression of which leads directly to our bloke world. "We have been laughing at their gay little madness, my dear, at their point-to-points, at the postural slump of the well-off and mentally underprivileged, at their stooping shoulders and strained accents, at their waffling cant, for so long . . . they are stupid, insensitive, unimaginative beyond hope, uncreative and murderous." The snarl and sarcasm and general offensiveness echo in the attitudes and work of the writers we are about to consider.

These days the bloke endures. He has given stiff competition as a social type to the old order, but also to the artist and intellectual, the academic, the large variety of countercultural types, the cool postmodernist, the rocker, the rapper, and the freak. His pugnacity and insight and capacity for pleasure make him vital. Whether he lives with integrity and decency is another matter. Whether he's any longer a first-class rambunctious man—or merely a tiresome hedonist, a British variation of a Hefner playboy—is a further question. In the years 2002–03, the BBC produced a series titled *Manchild*, the life and times of four fifty-something men in pursuit of women, drinks, camaraderie, and whatever it takes to escape the quotidian. The situation—edgy fun, risking oneself, asserting manliness—is a pop version of something that has been around . . . almost forever.

But the point is that these new men are at the center of the public imagination; the experiences they have are considered exemplary, worthy of close scrutiny, not merely the comic antics of minor players in a drama about more important people. The unseriousness, carelessness, and awfulness of these fellows are as significant as dignity once was for the gentleman. But *Manchild* is bloke lite, a fizzy entertainment with plenty of good acting and easy laughs. The pure levity is quite different from the significance that the bloke once had and continues to have in the best creative work of our time. The bloke writers considered in this book have much more searching things to say about maleness, the battle against mediocrity, class and its discontents. Before we take our men one by one, let's look back—way back—at some bloke ancestors. Although the character of our 1950s and 1960s men is shaped by their times, their way of being Englishmen has a back story.

The word bloke is shrouded in mystery: it could be of Celtic origin (a large person) or it could be Hindu; the *Oxford English Dictionary* will only yield up a couple of references from the Victorian age, with nothing more than uninteresting quotations. A bloke was evidently an ordinary male or even a low person. The word has nothing whatever to do with the extreme put-down terms churl and villain of the middle ages; it seeks to denote someone who is not high up in the esteem system, not a gentleman or a swell. But this inconspicuous ordinariness had its own power.

Begin in the fourteenth century if you're looking for the representation of the hedonistic, alive, and aggressive male. Chaucer's young students in his two famous fabliaux—"The Miller Tale" and "The Reeve's Tale"—are blokes before the word existed. Blokes are not louts or lowlifes like the Miller himself. Chaucer's Miller is a gross, drunken, down-and-dirty fellow who wants to upset the applecart on the way to Canterbury by telling a tale that violates all the standards upheld by the best medieval people. His behavior is an affront to the knight's chivalry, to courtly love, to gentleness, but the tale that he tells has a featured character who is far above the narrator in intelligence, insight, wit, love of fun, and desire to get his way. Nicholas—"hende" or clever—is an Oxford student with an interest in astronomy, a gift for harp playing and singing, a smooth presentation, and a nicely appointed bachelor chamber. He's a boarder in the house of a lout, an ignorant old man who has a young lecherous wife. True to the pattern of many blokes, he twists the code of the gentleman out of shape: he is discreet and secret in his pursuit of the young woman, very much like a courtly lover, yet lacking in delicacy and gentleness. His approach is direct and physical, with some sighing and pleading added in; his strategy for pursuing the affair is hilariously under-handed and far from the stock deceptions of the courtly lover. He devises an absurd scenario to trick the old man: the end of the world is at hand, says the astronomy student, and we have to pre-pare. Nicholas goes about his funny business with the young wife while the old codger prepares for a second deluge. Meanwhile bare bottoms, tubs of water, humiliation, fun poked at courtliness and fanciness are the ingredients of a tale that upends manners and civilization. True, Nicholas gets his backside burned with a hot poker, but he also gets his way with a rich man's wife and has plenty of fun convulsing the social order. His brains have made the fun, not his physical prowess, his character, or virtue. Forward to "The Reeve's Tale," a different version of the bloke's triumph. The ingredients are the same—witty, raunchy students, available females, a screwy plot to trick someone with wealth. This time the scene involves Cambridge and the students are notable for their Northern speech, even then the antithesis of gentlemanly polish and the source of a good laugh for Chaucer's audience. Alan and John, like Nicholas, are poor and full of tricks and jokes to com-pensate for their poverty. They sign on to take the college grain to the dishonest Miller, which is to say that they will fix him good with one of their best blokish performances. The Miller's daugh-ter, a bit of an eyesore but his prize possession, is relieved of her virginity by Alan in a late night scene of musical beds; his wife also gets a good time, planned by John. John's philosophy is not subtle, but it's perfectly in keeping with our theme of male assertion: "If in one point a person be aggrieved / Then in another he shall be relieved." Getting your own back is central to bloke life. It's the opposite of high-mindedness and high principle.

That isn't to say our men are purely reactive, without a code and a standard of their own. It takes wit, edge, and a real point of view to be a well-developed bloke. The resistant powers of the bloke are as strong as those of the gentleman—perhaps stronger. He stands out while gentlemen fit in. The Renaissance version in England is best seen in the character of Shakespeare's Falstaff, a man whose unmeltable selfhood rings down the centuries and overshadows the gentility of many a hero. Falstaff's objects in life are to face down obstacles with the fatness of his person ("turning his vices into commodity"), trump honor and glory with vitality and endurance, make the pursuit of pleasure an infinitely clever pastime. The perdurable self—its wants and whims—is the paramount thing. And don't ask why. "If reasons were as plentiful as blackberries, I would give no man a reason upon compulsion." We, however, see what it's all about: braving death ("do not bid me remember mine end," he says to Doll Tearsheet), mocking dreary circumstances and people (including army recruits with names like Simon Shadow, Thomas Wart, Francis Feeble), and breaking out of boundaries. These last include the obligations of gentle birth, the claims of honesty, the limits of one's environment. Debts are unpaid, old geezer friends are insulted (Shallow is a very genius of famine, a cheese paring, a forked radish), lies are joyfully retailed. To be, to enjoy, to survive—and to do so with the stamp of one's own cleverness. Hazlitt, a man we will consider presently, was on the mark when he explained the precise nature of Falstaff's wit. "His body is like a good estate to his mind, from which he receives rents and revenues of profit and pleasure in kind." Wit can often be a meager thing, a "substitute" for "pleasurable sensation." But not with Falstaff; in his case it's a "giving vent to his heart's ease and over-contentment with himself and others. . . . The secret of Falstaff's wit is for the most part a masterly presence of mind, an absolute self-possession, which nothing can disturb." There's nothing above this ease and self-possession—which is at once exciting and disturbing and part of our larger story of the bloke's run in literary culture.

Henry Fielding's Tom Jones is the next bloke in line, an affront to the decencies of his time—Dr. Johnson was shocked—and a founding father of modern instinct, fun, and freedom from the limits of propriety. The Victorians—even as manly a writer as Thackeray—were censorious about his amorous activities; but a century later Tom was the most likeable of protagonists in Tony Richardson's enormously successful film. John Osborne's screenplay—called a "marvel" by critic Jonathan Yardley—is perfectly faithful to the spirit of the book, to its hilarious campaign against cant, dreariness, and hypocrisy. English awfulness—Mr. Blifil's sanctimoniousness, Mr. Thwackum's brutality—is pitted against the fresh, randy, vital honesty of Tom. Tom of course was a picaro, that wild boy of the early novel who had adventures, took a great many risks, and was a source of entertainment to the gentry but not quite the ticket as a role model. Other eighteenth century novelists such as Defoe and Smollett who dealt with misadventures and the wild side of life were considered funny and instructive and piquant but in the long run rather low. Smollett's Humphrey Clinker and others with his profile were not heroic or exalted or decorous or gentlemanly or anything that the age of Dr. Johnson gave much credit to. What they were was amusing and instructive and piquant.

The romantic age offered the elemental emotions of simple people as one of its selling points: beggars, rustic workers, men tied to arduous circumstance, and country living got a major place in English literature because so much time had been spent of late on the sublime and the abstract. But Wordsworth and Burns didn't go far with the raw spirit of ordinariness and the suffering that attended it. "A Man's a Man for a' that" might be a famous line of the era, but it didn't count for much. Men of low station who had to contend with the awfulness of their lot were by and large a polite group. Leech gatherers and Cumberland beggars and the like were as civil as vicars. Sneering and mocking and ranting were more to be found on the aristocratic side of the movement.

But in the 1820s the romantic essayist William Hazlitt seemed to be getting out of line in a number of ways. He had the ingredients that make for a strong, resistant social type, a literary man outside the gentlemanly bounds. He was intellectually powerful without being a product of the universities, interesting as a personality although socially nowhere in a land of delicate hierarchical distinctions, and sexually bold. He offered a new brand of pushfulness, with his own nature at the center. He was a critic and observer of everyday life—juggling acts, prize fights, new art, and writing. He made his attitude—a restless, street-wise pursuit of beauty and truth in the arts and living—into a spectacle: he popularized the word "gusto," and used the textured story of his own enjoyments, sensuous observations, and misadventures to describe the artistic mission. In doing so, he championed a social type, best depicted in his essay "The Fight." At an inn on the way to a boxing match he met a fellow who suited his tastes, was bored with convention and routine, and used the word "insipid" in just the right way. "He was a fine fellow, with sense, wit, and spirit, and a hearty body and joyous mind, free-spoken, frank and convivial—one of that true English breed that went with Harry to Harfleur." In his 1822 essay "On the Pleasure of Hating" he talks further about the insipid, all that drives you crazy in daily life and opinion; he shows the ways in which negativity, exasperation and aggression, disgust, and defiance stir us up, spare us the stagnant life all around us, give us a defense against the platitudes of rationalists and the decorum of gentlemen. A sometime pal, John Keats, described Hazlitt this way: "Hazlitt has damned the bigoted and blue-stockinged; how durst the man? He is your only good damner, and if ever I am damned—damn me if I shouldn't like him to dam me." He cries out against "Legitimacy," which is to say the political repressions of his era; but the political point—he was a lover of Napoleon in a country that had given its all to defeat the heritage of the French Revolution—is not quite the full story. He's a writer who wants to separate us from the settled order and calmness, whether in manners or artistic judgment. "The greatest possible good of each individual consists in doing all the mischief he can to his neighbors." The man and critic is constantly on guard against the worn-out—anything he might be sick of, including the raunchy classic *Tom Jones*. "Lest it should not answer my expectations at this time of day . . . I should certainly be disposed to fling it into the fire."

He lived the life that perfectly fits this, complete with the money troubles and the refusal to be nice according to the public sexual standards of the period. He wasn't simply the focus of scandal like Lord Byron; he was a writer who gave a true-life account of his flirtation-sensual affair with a girl who was the daughter of his landlady. Sarah Walker—a minx—became the most important person in the life of a critic, and he told his readership (a literary readership!) openly about fondling her, agonizing over her other lovers, even talking about the affair with her parents. The whole thing, published as *Liber Amoris*, is one of the greatest texts in the history of mortification, but also just the thing that a bloke would want: the force of his desire meeting every kind of misfortune and showing itself up as immovable. He's surely the angry young man of his era, as J. B. Priestley has noted in his book—angry about class, love gone wrong, and public dreariness.

Late in the next decade the bloke was at the center of English literature. In the tenth chapter of *The Pickwick Papers* a nice retired gentleman named Samuel Pickwick meets a future employee named Sam Weller. Mr. Pickwick wants to travel and observe English life at leisure and he could use a manservant. What he gets is one of the greatest comic, transgressive mouths in our language. Sam's a Cockney, which is to say hold the illusions and the niceties. He's streetwise, the son of a coachman who also has a fund of wisdom and usually a certain number of drinks taken. Father and son are masters of resistance: they put up a fight against the whole world of insipidity and convention that Hazlitt described. Sam has, according to one scholar, sixty some odd verbal shots directed at things in general. They're gags, nervy observations about man and society that have the originator's twist and the shape of his personality. ("That's what I call a self-evident proposition, as the dog's meat man said, when the housemaid told him he warn't a gentleman.") The public in Dickens's time went crazy for these Wellerisms—and they have become a permanent part of Dickens's comic achievement. But it wasn't easy to create such a spontaneous bloke; later humorously drawn servants such as Mark Tapley in *Martin Chuzzlewit* are pretty tedious. Dickens lashed out perfectly once in the comic vein, setting a great standard of irrepressibility. Mr. Pickwick, all innocence and reserve, tries to rein Sam in, but don't count on the results. Dickens himself was socially ambitious—wanted to be a gentleman—but in novel after novel he was unafraid of offending just about every socially important or merely respectable type of his era. Some Sam Weller in him wouldn't shut up about merchants and bankers and counting house owners and big men on the exchange and aristocratic do-nothings (not to mention their ladies). And Dickens got the reputation for being a bit below the mark as a thinker and observer, someone who didn't have a grasp of the life and ways of the better educated and genteel: even Carlyle, a radical who liked him, condescendingly referred to little Boz (Dickens's penname from his first book of sketches). To many, Dickens was rather common—and to Bloomsbury in the next century he would be unspeakably out of it with his pushy flat characters who had stock lines of dialogue. But Dickens lovers have always countered by championing the teeming humanity of his books rather than the subtlety.

His people explode with life—vulgar, vicious, kindly, cruel, and crazy. They seize you in a Shakespearean way.

Dickens wrote furiously for several decades, caring very little about the niceties of craft. His main concern was to finish long tales about his society, to avoid the tedious, and to communicate with his readers. He wanted to be a smashing figure and to compensate himself for personal unhappiness. The well-known history of his childhood days in a blacking factory is enough to establish him as a writer whose imagination was charged by resentment and pain from the start. His major images of British awfulness and inhumanity—in the workhouses, the vile South of London tenements, the dumping ground boarding schools, the mill towns, the grim counting houses, even the bleak Sunday London streets—are about being ground under. He had a great talent for evoking threats to the self. And he knew how to sustain his rage in book after book.

The same can be said for that other bloke, Rudyard Kipling. He made his name by being an observer of strugglers in the army and their sharp and ungenteel idiom. But he developed a kind of disreputable philosophy of power and strength—bullying your bullies—that resonated with many a British man. He wrote for put-down people who weren't so much socialist in their sympathies as sick of it all, frustrated and confused. His first big literary success, *Barrack Room Ballads,* was meant to be an in-your-face treatment of the British soldier's travails, the condition of being a nobody in a world of somebodies and of having to listen to all the hot air of public opinion and endure all the cold shoulder. His men were the rag-tag characters that kept the Empire together and he intended to give you the picture. It was a job that he executed with tremendous force, rhythmic skill, dictional color, and rhetorical power—giving famous lines to English verse and a sense of autonomy and male self-worth to many. He saw the nasty side of life, and that made the pluck and grit less sentimental. It was a heady brew. He got himself into no end of trouble with bullying and what seems like proto-fascism; but he did so in the name of not letting people be ground down. An impolite complainer with a forceful collection of social beliefs and a sometimes funny poetic idiom, he could amuse and arrest.

Barrack Room Ballads, considering the decorum of the age, is a bit raw—frank about drunkenness, meanness and cruelty, sexiness in Mandalay and blah in Britain ("There's a Burma girl a-settin' and I know she thinks of me" makes the "beefy" faced housemaids from Chelsea seem pretty unappealing.) And all around are impolite accounts of what it's like to live according to the British way. The state of things is well summed up in "Tommy"—little wars that are needed for Empire and little men who are considered good enough to serve but not good enough to be decently treated. They're also to be praised with hot air rhetoric in times of crisis: "Thin red line of heroes when the drums begin to roll." But mostly barrack life is about lying in your own defeat like the speaker of "Cells": "I've a mouth like an old potato and I'm more than a little sick." "I've had my fun," which is to say blackened the corporal's eye, been thrown in the clink for "Drunk and resisting the Guard." The porter and beer and measure of gin didn't cause the incident. "There was an extry double guard that rubbed my nose in the dirt." And with Kipling there's always someone or something beating down on you—even "the Widow at Windsor." "For 'alf o' Creation she owns: / "We 'ave brought 'er the same with the sword and the flame / An' we've salted it down with our bones."

The most famous poems in the volume, "Danny Deever" and "Gunga Din," deal with pain in an almost metaphysical way: what can be done for it? Kipling's blokes honor it by making us watch its dramatic unfolding. Deever, "a sneakin' shootin' hound," shot a man in his bed and deserves what he's getting. But the brutality of the execution—rendered through the chilling details of the ballad form—make us as readers face the raw mystery of someone else's plight. That someone was awful but human. "'E's sleepin' out an' far to-night," the Colour-Sergeant said. Files-on-Parade has drunk "'is beer a score of times." But as Colour-Sergeant says, "'E's drinkin' bitter beer tonight." Kipling has the right phrases to scare us and curiously brace us up. In the scheme of things—from which there is no way out—"they're done with Danny Deever, you can hear the quickstep play." But ironically this thug will stand as an image of what the army can produce: his fate will make young recruits tremble and need their beer. They'll remember the bits of comradeship along with the horror. The poem is probably one of the most famous British lessons ever in taking it. And "Gunga Din" is the other: the ragged regimental bhisti of the title "didn't seem to know the use o' fear." Depicted as a phenomenon of energy, alertness, compassion, and care, "You're a better man than I am, Gunga Din." You meet standards of hardihood and resistance that I can't meet. You're not quite heroic—for that we'd have to have you singled out. We'll meet in hell some day where you'll be giving drink to poor damned souls.

Literary modernism had little use for Kipling's anger and commitment to the average bloke. It was from the beginning looking for the truths of human life in the consciousness of the artist, the writer, the oddball, the extraordinary observer. True enough, blokes and their central problem—being overwhelmed by class, money, and change—were brilliantly treated by Joyce in *Dubliners*: his angry young clerks, street toughs, and nowhere men who want something are shown in various states of paralysis. But the life-availing part of Joyce's masculine world is about very different things: art, enriched sexuality, and curiosity about nature and society. And the hard, aggressive side of bloke life is nowhere to be found in Joyce's superbly ordinary man, Leopold Bloom. Bloom occupies big territory, perhaps beyond the bloke's reach. In any case Joseph Conrad, E. M. Forster, James Joyce, and D. H. Lawrence all produced early books that seemed to care little for the old kind of resistance—it wasn't the old manners, conventions, hierarchies, and fustiness that kept you down; look instead to limits that the mind imposes, to the smallness of ideologies, to the power of the subconscious mind, to the ironies of love and devotion gone wrong. Discover new territory and new form to express it. The old Dickensian gripes have grown old, and his books have ceased to startle.

But Lawrence the modernist—which is to say bold experimenter—showed how the bloke endured as a figure of significance in the age of Woolf, Conrad, and Joyce. He was a daring Nottingham boy who practiced many literary forms (being an exquisite craftsman in the short story) and also focused on rough characters who wanted freedom from insipidity—sexual and social. They often had big mouths and explosive tempers. Their words were far from polite, far from the impassioned but urbane protest about society delivered in E. M. Forster's *Howards End*. The tone of the Cambridge Common Room and the reasoned pursuit of beauty and intellectual gratification associated with Bloomsbury writers such as Forster, Woolf, and the philosopher G. E. Moore was nowhere to be found in Lawrence. This modernist bluntly and fiercely said new things about British awfulness and argued about manliness. While Moore's *Principia Ethica* made Bloomsbury men studiously mild and critical and urbane in evaluating life, Lawrence tore into problems about living in a way that had none of the fine-spun irony and distance from common experience characteristic of the newer writers. He was basic about the old issue of being ground down, and in a new way since he was open about bad sex and bad civilization. In the books in which he contributed to the modernist revolution, he was trying to incorporate his sense of maleness and how it constituted an adventure and an escape from the dreary arrangements of his society.

Sons and Lovers was published three years after *Howards End* but its picture of what the modern aggressive male was getting out of life in terms of emotional gratification is vastly different. The vulgar swagger and pleasure of Charles Wilcox—complete with a careless disregard for little people who led little lives—doesn't make it seem as if he has much heart or sense. His father Henry is no better, despite intelligence. Forward to Paul Morel, that miner's son who is alert enough from the start to know what's beautiful and horrible in England. Paul is half-mother's child (quick mental life and spiritual awareness) and half father's (instinct and sensitivity to bodily sensation). But he wants to turn against the former and become a new person: he'd like to stop being nice for a while and live like Morel. He tells his mother—the woman who made him get an education and pursue his painting—that he actually liked the whole world of men and machines and manual labor that she turned him against. When she asks him if he'd he satisfied with his dad's pals down at the pub, the answer is far from clear. Yes, Paul can bond with Baxter Dawes, a roughneck whose wife Clara Paul has seduced. Baxter gives Paul a terrible beating, but don't worry; it doesn't make Paul a poor sport. They have shared a woman, and Paul goes to see his old comrade in passion when the latter is sick. But the last part of the book turns away from the comfort of talking to another bloke and gets back to where we started—choosing. There's something wrong with the Morel-Dawes picture—not enough in common. Yet Lawrence isn't using this bloke scene for no reason: he's after a vague but deeply held belief about the power of the British male of humble origins.

Blokes in Lawrence are part of a great escape team, saving people from the awfulness of conventional life. Since Lawrence knew their worst side from the drinking and brawling of his father, he also didn't mind adding cruelty and aggression to their vitality. The bloke could be a bit of a bully in the cause of liberation: in order to change things for himself—escape the fate of the industrial society victim—he had to have hardness at the ready, including strategies and tough talk. In Lawrence he wants something or someone: he wants desire and full possession of another's being. "You Touched Me" is about two sisters who have been raised by a rich father at his pottery works. Years before he had adopted a charity boy to raise up, a Cockney kid who never really fit in or liked the genteel sisters. He went his way in Canada for a time and then came back when the old man was dying: an adventurer for sure, no gentleman, not a trace of niceness in him outside his pally manner with the dying man. But in a scene of stunning impact he feels the sensual touch of one of the sisters; she accidentally stroked him one night when there was a confusion of his room and the father's. And off he goes from there, refusing to give up on someone who touched him. This instinctual reaction must govern everything, and he forces her (through her father's will) to marry. Not pretty, but also not conventional. Another low grade Lawrence bloke is the pick-up artist in "Tickets, Please." He likes thrills, flirtations, outings at the Statutes fair—and then the next girl. He's been choosing among the tram conductor girls, and one of them, Annie, has enough pluck to get the girls to gang up and symbolically violate their victimizer. The trouble is she still feels something for him—even in his pathetic final state.

Other stories treat a better class of bloke and are more serious about bloke power, love of vital living, and desire and passion. Take the "prince" bloke in "The Horse Dealer's Daughter," a doctor who saves a girl (in Cinderella style) from . . . well, family coldness. A victim of two loutish brothers, poor Mabel—about to lose her home—has tried to drown herself. The doctor, seeing her sink under in a pond, pulls her back to life. Her savior winds up moving from compassion and professionalism to passion. He also winds up finding what he wants. Besides saving her, he has also liberated the two of them from the predictable, from the conventions governing the lives of single women and from his own sense of what a doctor should be like. "Jimmy and the Desperate Woman" philosophizes about the eternal question of how a fellow can get a share of good things in a crushing world. It's a meditation—told in the form of a romantic adventure—on what you'll need to consider and do if you want passion. Jimmy is the editor of a high-end literary journal, a recent divorcé, and a very handsome catch whom his friends regard as a satyr. His ex-wife regarded him as a bit of a wimp. ("If he could only stand alone for ten minutes.") He determines to meet a "real" woman, not a literary sophisticate—maybe a girl out of Thomas Hardy. An isolated female contributor sends poems through the mail and we're soon into a story about what it takes to stand up to Mrs. Pinnegar, a tall beauty who has been bullied by her miner husband and cheated on because she won't be submissive. The husband is by no means a lout, however; he's a voice out of Kipling, one that can shout back at the citified editor. The journals and all the smart people "get you nowhere." Jimmy of course fires back, "Where do you want to get?" Pinnegar's answer is a non sequitur, that is until you get the flow. "I'm a man, aren't I?" He won't be used and ground under. To which Jimmy adds that "we're all used, from King George downwards. We have to be. When you eat your pudding you're making use of hundreds of people—including your wife." That's not the end of it though because Pinnegar wants submission from a wife as compensation for the harshness of his existence. This is cruel, but all-too-human, the Kiplingesque bloke getting back at everything in a stupid way. Jimmy, however, has a huge adventure on his hands, a desperate woman (with her child), and the incredible swoon that she produces. The sensation is like "neat whisky."

Lawrence makes his gamekeeper Mellors, the protagonist of *Lady Chatterley's Lover*, someone who can accept the challenge of what scares Jimmy. He's a very curious amalgam of the bloke and the gentleman—being a man of the working classes with a grammar school education, down to earth yet able to communicate on an intellectual level, gentle yet capable of brutality and vulgarity of the Walter Morel sort. He's more bloke than gent just because of this latter rawness, earthiness, and anger. He's the extreme version of our type, stretched out of shape really by Lawrencian primitivism and utopianism. Lawrence's gamekeeper would remake the world along the lines of private passion and tenderness. Criticism of the British social order, desire for personal risk and adventure, visions of a sexual future of liberation combine to make the book a lunatic proposal for happiness. Even Lawrence knows he's asking for too much. Most blokes in English literary history have been less feral than Mellors—less frighteningly physical and lacking in conventionality; and yet we must pause reverently before him and acknowledge that he gave male power enduring imaginative form in the first third of the twentieth century.

Don't look for powerful blokes in the novels of Graham Greene or Evelyn Waugh, those two successors to the great generation of British modernists from the teens. A curious out of step young gentleman—actually not quite accepted as a gentleman at his prep school—was to fill in the next chapter of the bloke's story: George Orwell—whom everyone knows was born plain Eric Blair—had an extended tale to tell about feelings of social injury that seemed to come from school, upbringing, Imperial service. He sometimes used his own life, sometimes thinly disguised scenes. He stayed on two topics in his finest essays: the power of the stubborn individual refusing to play the familiar and often horrible games of his century and the sufferings inflicted on those being ground under by new and old ideologies and administrations. He used his personal experience as the victim of a system as the motivation for a career in literary getting-back: like Dickens and Kipling, he assumed the point of view of the oppressed because he himself had been oppressed. "Such, Such Were the Joys"—the story of prep school life at a place called Crossgates—is about learning that you're not made for success. Put plainly, he was "not a good type of boy"; academic achievement in winning a couple of public school scholarships didn't change the fact that Blair was not in possession of what his little society and his masters valued: "I did not possess character or courage or health or strength or money, or even good manners, the power to look like a gentleman." He claimed he looked ugly and probably smelt. The response to all this was a lifelong attack on "unalterable law." By using the phrase from Milton, Orwell wanted to convey his scorn for social privileges and fashionable practices—and all the censoring and cruelty that were built into upholding them. It was a kind of loose-jointed war against "them": all the smart and well-born and moneyed and their political friends and Imperial connections. This war against being ground down extended to other oppressors, ones who were less easy to identify—the dreary, gray, respectable middle classes that he depicted in *Keep the Aspidistra Flying*. And there were also mass culture and ideology starting to have their effects—which brought every kind of contempt for the integrity of language. Words became contemptible playthings, either euphemisms or political lies and cover-ups. The "readymade phrases" described in "Politics and the English Language" are what enrage Orwell. In one way or the other he showed himself—or a figure very like himself—trying to put up a resistance to most of the phrases of his time. "The Art of Donald Magill"—about the subversive power of vulgar seaside postcards—is also about the inner bloke in Orwell, the rude part of him that refused to listen to cant. "I never read the proclamations of generals before battle, the speeches of führers and prime ministers, the solidarity songs of public schools and Left wing political parties, national anthems, Temperance tracts, papal encyclicals and sermons against gambling and contraception, without seeming to hear in the background a chorus of raspberries from all the millions of common men to whom these high sentiments make no appeal."

In "Why I Write" Orwell described his own blend of the aesthetic and the political: the feeling for language, sounds, effects went as deep as his being and could not be detached from his desire to get back at the awfulness of carelessly used language. It was essentially the lone man defying the mystifiers, the ideologues, the catchphrase makers—and, yes, artists with their excessive faith in art. Such a writing philosophy made Orwell an exemplary figure, an old-fashioned bringer of clarity in an age of ambiguity. He drew people to his essentially democratic/socialist outlook by showing them his brand of forcefulness: he would stand up for decency and not being ground down. He'd oppose everything else—every orthodoxy, slogan, and rallying cry.

In his book on the great essayist, Christopher Hitchens creates a bridge of sorts between Orwell the political writer and Philip Larkin the poet of private feeling. Interestingly enough the young poet introduced the well-known writer at an Oxford Democratic and Socialist Club and English Club meeting in 1941; Orwell delivered a talk called "Literature and Totalitarianism." Hitchens reminds us that Larkin liked Orwell's writing and goes on to create some fine appositions between these two men—the melancholy "greensward and greystone," the eye for local detail, the directness. But Hitchens does not emphasize the fact that both these writers were aggressive promoters of a new position in British literary culture: they wanted a new kind of artistic freedom, one that the Depression and war years could not give them. Orwell, the writer known for his battle against the Thought Police, wrote an essay in 1940 that strangely seemed to direct writers away from optimism about society and culture, away from humanistic values and tradition. He told them to get "inside the whale," which is to say to ignore the dreams of art and culture of the 1930s. Culture was hopeless in an age of barbarity. We have no need of Joyce, but of Henry Miller with his fiddling while Rome burns—with his face toward the flames. When the modern movement's great figures were dying off, Orwell also had nothing bracing to say about them. It was as if nothing had fallen when Joyce and Yeats and Woolf had left us. The important thing was to get inside the whale—to see the uselessness of art and try to survive.

The young Larkin took very little from the political and cultural upheaval of his time, preferring to write about his own moods and frustrations: his first significant work was the novel *Jill*, about unhappy days at Oxford, snobbery, and lashing out at "them," the swells at his college. He was—inevitably—caught in the austerities of the war, but he and a number of other writers of his time didn't seem to be caught up in literary modernism. Malcolm Bradbury has said that for these young writers who came on in the 1940s, VJ meant victory over Joyce and VE victory over Eliot. They were after a kind of freedom that was not modernist freedom. The central thing about them seemed to be their outbursts: aggression, play, and candor that had almost nothing to do with stream of consciousness or symbolism and everything to do with the male character and the life of a country struggling to make its way after a costly victory.

2

Philip Larkin

Philip Larkin is in the great tradition of English resistance. He refused to make peace with gentility, niceness, reassuring messages, good taste, and contemporary fashion. His life and work were informed by an offensiveness—in word and attitude—that makes him a controversial figure for the new millennium: he would have hated being called transgressive (too trendy by half), but as a poet and man he violated most of the conventions and defied the expectations of his time and ours. Although he spent many years as a super-efficient librarian and top administrator—not to mention two decades as a famous writer—he purposefully failed most of the tests of modern life: he was never married, but chose a life of philandering without the glamour of the rake; he was a heavy drinker without being a bon vivant or anecdote-inspiring drunk; he was resistant to pop culture, contemporary literature—everything lively and new except the jazz of his youth; he was sarcastic and doleful in the age of rock 'n' roll and the Beatles; he was a perpetual old man without the eccentric style of an Evelyn Waugh; he was a poet of craftsmanship and small output who lacked the spontaneous, overflowing, spirit-driven qualities of famous poets of his era such as Lowell, Ginsberg, Hughes, or Plath. He wasn't in the grip of a great instinctual talent; he could write poetry—or stop for years. He was, as the speaker in one of his poems puts it, "one of those old-type *natural* fouled-up guys." But that isn't to say he was conventional: from the start of his writing life as a teenager, he was, like Brando in *The Wild One*, rebelling against whatever was around. And in his maturity, with his horn-rimmed glasses, formal manner, and dark suits, he raised hell in English literature by refusing the role of the public man and performer, the London swinger, or the poet-sage. He embraced the ordinary, the doldrums where most people live with unfashionable boredom and fear. If he struck a pose, it was that of the irritable, slightly depressed bloke—unenthusiastic about political movements, ideologies, the in-crowd's views of the arts and literature.

In his poem "Symphony in White Major," his persona lifts a very large gin and tonic to a "private pledge"—"*He devoted his life to others.*" Such a sentiment is undercut not only by the italics, but by irony in the rest of the poem, one line of which calls him "A brick, a trump, a proper sort." Larkin was nothing of the kind: he was an artist who was true to his flawed, self-absorbed nature. He expressed that often unattractive nature in poem after poem. And not only did he lack the conventional solidities and graces, he had little that was especially dramatic to write about. His life was one of the great anti-romantic stories in English literary history: no big struggles against poverty or family privilege, no country house isolation or hard times in a blacking factory, no eccentric mother or extravagant father, no drunken scenes in the home, no public school spirit or trauma, no communion with nature, no quaint surroundings or good architecture. In "I Remember, I Remember" the voice calls out "Why, Coventry!" and then proceeds to relate non-events in a nondescript place: the poem is in the emotional key of Flaubert's *Sentimental Education*—about life failing to happen. "Nothing, like something, happens anywhere." After centuries of exciting literary lives—from Milton to Byron to Dickens to Lawrence—Larkin's unsparkling life is a novelty of sorts. And nothing much is given many twists and variations by the artist, is viewed from many angles, is imbued with an unusual temperament, and transformed into fine poetry.

The Larkin household was entirely lacking in the rough-and-tumble of the lower middle and working classes. Larkin's father Sydney was a solid business success, an accountant who rose to become Treasurer of Coventry. He had been an honors student at King Edward High School and thereafter went on to the University of Birmingham where he passed demanding examinations. A tightly wound, disciplined young man, Sydney climbed the middle-class ladder that led to esteem as a financial administrator, provincial prosperity, a refined wife, and a detached house in the residential district of Coventry. He acquired culture as well. Sydney was a reader with an avid interest in modern literature and a taste for Shaw, Hardy, Bennett, Huxley—even Joyce and Lawrence. Philip's mother Eva had contemplated a life as a librarian, taught school for a time, and attracted a man who found her bookish nature—she was reading when he picked her up on holiday in Wales—to his taste. Eva was mousy and a lifetime whiner. Sydney was a brisk authoritarian. Their life—aside from his professional progress—had one big theme: the development of young Philip, his father's favorite. Philip's older sister counted for little in the family history, but the father's golden son—intellectual and literary, if not quite a model student—was carefully nurtured and treated with deference. Sydney was impatient with his wife, exacting on the job, but quite different with his son. He introduced the boy to the books he loved, talked about the fine points of language, was open to the youngster's interest in jazz, helped finance a set of drums, and generally soft-pedaled his tyrannical side. Larkin respected and admired his father and had a good deal of contempt for his complaining mother.

But Sydney's character had a dark side that Larkin was at pains to cover up. The pillar of Coventry and dedicated family man was an ardent admirer of Hitler during the 1930s; he had a small statuette of his hero at home which, when a button was pressed, gave the Nazi salute. He took young Philip on two trips to Germany in the late 1930s and expressed a deep respect for the organizational powers and order of the regime. Philip—a dazed teenager, according to Andrew Motion—didn't know what to think; yet later on he did his best to destroy any record of the paternal taste in politics. This was done with quiet resolve and nowhere in Larkin's letters and other writings is there any denunciation of his father's views. Larkin apparently had no delicacy of conscience or sense of duty that called for regret or guilt feelings.

But in other areas of life—sex, cultural tastes, literary preferences—Larkin soon became a master at complaining. From a home in which his father gave what Motion refers to as "crushing" orders and pronouncements and his mother whined about the trouble of running the establishment, Larkin developed into a strange sort of commander/complainer; one role seeped into the other and his grumblings became dictates. His identity was a matter of asserting a resistant self against school, then wartime Oxford, then the idea of the literary life, and then the conception of happiness.

Larkin wrote a letter to a school chum in 1939 that sets the tone for things to come: "Please believe me when I say that half my days are spent in black, surging, twitching, boiling HATE!!!" Home life—the uninteresting furniture, the whimpering and ordering, the boredom, the lack of family friends—must have played a part in making a boy define himself this way. But hate when used by teenagers, writers, and rhetoricians is not a purely destructive and life-denying emotion. In his essay "On Hating," Hazlitt well understood what the young Larkin was getting at: "Nature seems (the more we look into it) made up of antipathies: without something to hate, we should lose the very spring of thought and action. Life would turn to a stagnant pool, were it not ruffled by the jarring interests, the unruly passions of men." Larkin was battling against stagnation. At King Henry VIII School, the local grammar school where Larkin was enrolled at eight, he slacked off, got the reputation of being a sly rebel, and spent time writing plays, stories, and "diatribes against various things such as education and Christianity." He found a pal named Jim Sutton, an intense type, very literary, and a jazz enthusiast: "friends are necessary: you can't howl at yourself," Larkin said. Aside from English, he neglected his studies, and didn't come alive until the 6th Form, at which point he had a knowledge of Eliot, Auden, and French Symbolism. He had too uneven a record for a scholarship to university, and Sydney could well afford to pay. An exam taker, he gained his place at St John's, Oxford.

Oxford during the war was drab, lacked the glamour of the *Brideshead* generation or the intellectual and political ferment of the Auden years. No antics of aesthetes like Brian Howard and Harold Acton; no champagne and plover's eggs at luncheon parties. Also no Communist meetings, heated arguments, comrades vs. solid Englishmen. Andrew Motion called the 1940s at the University "a life on rations." Larkin profiled it in a letter to a friend: the "axis had been shaken from the Radcliffe Camera to Carfax"; army lorries "thunder" and shoppers queue. No "high living"—"You had one bottle of wine a term from the buttery—that was your lot." Resistant Larkin decided to bring a taste of the outrageous to a world that was doing its bit for the war effort; he dressed dandiacally in bow ties, green or red slacks—and added his outsize horn rims. But the fanciness was combined with a totally anti-Establishment taste in friends and culture.

Larkin had a holy horror of public school types—perhaps coming from his up-from-the-ranks father and certainly coming from the pride of the grammar school boy who was every bit as smart as the well born. People in his year ticked him off: "their public school accent renders them incapable of saying anything interesting or amusing. No intelligent man uses the public school accent for the simple reason that one simply cannot say intelligent things in it. That is a *fact*." But to make this declaration a part of his life he went to great lengths in seeking out the wrong people. Norman Iles, a Bristol Grammar School boy at St John's, was the ticket. He had a regional accent, a rough presentation, and a to-hell-with-it attitude toward all the conventional things. Larkin used him as a "means of weighing up my characters and assumptions. Any action or even word implying respect for qualities such as punctuality, prudence, thrift or respectability called forth a snarling roar like that of the Metro-Goldwyn-Mayer lion." Larkin and Iles met through their tutor, a reserved scholar of Anglo-Saxon who hadn't long to live and treated the boys with forbearance. Larkin said the two of them seemed like "village idiots who might if tried hard turn nasty." Their mockery, border-line boorishness, and lack of studiousness were, apparently, the latest thing in the protest line: the *Brideshead* generation had scorned college hearties and cultivated an aesthete manner; the Auden generation was argumentative and intensely analytic about the social condition of England. These new undergraduates were blunt, somewhat philistine, rather surly: they seemed to sigh at the prospect of literary tradition and high culture. Larkin, the writer who was one day to be famous for his direct, Anglo-Saxon diction, couldn't stand the study of Old English, hated J. R. R. Tolkien's and C. S. Lewis's lectures, and referred to *Beowulf* and the Anglo-Saxon works in the curriculum as "ape's bum fodder." Soon he was to meet another pal through Iles. Kingsley Amis specialized in antic behavior of a buffoonish sort, heavy drinking, and relentless irreverence. Larkin and Amis teamed up and did their best to deflate and denigrate the standard authors and standard Oxford manners. Amis is the recording secretary of their blokish literary commentary and parody. The Romantic poets became a jazz group called the Hot Six with Wordsworth (tmb) and Johnny Keats (alto, clt). Larkin wrote against romanticism in a parody of Shelley—"Music when soft *silly* voices, that have been talking *piss* die, Vibrates like a . . ." There's also this send-up of Keats: "And this is why I shag alone / Ere half my creeping days are done." Crude and rude when he spotted conventional beauty in a college copy of *The Eve of St. Agnes*, he glossed "Into her dream he melted" with "YOU MEAN HE FUCKED HER." Andrew Motion has collected the choice bits of such stuff, including that *The Faerie Queen* is "the dullest thing out. Blast it." Canonical literature was generally pompous, dreary, filled with circumlocutions. "Art is awfully wrong, you know," Larkin wrote to another friend.

Excitement came from listening to jazz, getting pissed at the pub or in college rooms, and loving the high priest of spontaneity, D. H. Lawrence. Real relations with girls were in Larkin's future: at Oxford there was plenty of bawdy talk, masturbatory fantasizing, but zero action. He spent hours listening carefully to the Blues artists of the 1930s—especially Armstrong, Waller, and Beiderbecke—and thereafter made them the center of his conversations with Amis; years later he deposited his responses to jazz in his essays, collected in 1970 in a volume titled *All What Jazz*.

From the start the complaining and commanding pattern applied to this passion: he couldn't stand jazz men who let virtuosity overcome feeling and visceral pleasure. Jazz was a way of tapping into the instinctual life; for Larkin it had been a matter of playing his drums to the sounds of the artists of the day, banging away on toffee tins, and banishing the world of school. At Oxford it took up enough time to threaten his academic work: long hours in fellow undergraduates' rooms listening and moving to the sounds seemed more significant than long hours in the library. When he came to write about this immersion in pure feeling, he wanted it known that pleasure and joy and escape were the sources of appeal. *All What Jazz* explains that jazz and the modernist movement in literature, jazz as a head trip for highbrows, jazz without catchy tunes and lyrics meant nothing to him. He couldn't stand the pyrotechnics of Parker or Coletrane. For him the problem was the barrenness of modernism: "This is my essential criticism of modernism, whether perpetrated by Parker, Proust or Picasso: it helps us neither to enjoy nor endure."

We are "mystified or outraged" by technically difficult works, but we are not braced up or given sustenance. His reaction to Sidney Bechet's music in a letter to his friend Jim Sutton is totally without any discriminating power, but totally heart-felt. The young man who sneered at Shelley's outpourings didn't realize that his own shout-out was romanticism in the raw: "Fucking, cunting, bloody good." He said the same thing—but elegantly—in "For Sidney Bechet": "On me your voice falls as they say love should, / Like an enormous yes." For all Larkin's derogating of the modernist movement, that yes sounds like Molly Bloom.

"Good steady drinking," Motion reports, meant six pints a night. "Dockery and Son," Larkin's best poem about Oxford, shows the consequences with the authorities: "remember how / Blackgowned, unbreakfasted, and still half tight / We used to stand before that desk to give / 'Our version' of 'these incidents last night'?" Hard drinking was nothing new at Oxford, but Larkin's gleeful shamelessness was. No claret-soaked sophistication and bon mots for him. On vacation he writes to a friend of his mode of living and working: he's "shitting about Warwick," swilling his (only) two pints a night, writing "crappy" poems, and yearning for a voice of his own—not something out of Pound or Joyce. When he speaks of Auden—with high praise—he likens him to jazzman Pee Wee Russell. He's a belligerent drunk who uses Middle English to speak of a "sodynge good kyk in the balles" delivered to a friend "at which I hadde grate merriment." Larkin much enjoyed the spectacle of Dylan Thomas at the University, getting his own back at the literary establishment: "little, snubby, hopelessly pissed bloke who made hundreds of cracks and read parodies of everybody in appropriate voices." The "cracks" were what meant most in the long run. Literature for Larkin was part of bloke life. He and his pals formed a literary group called "The Seven," intentionally meant to exclude scholars and intellectuals who offended their anti-academic spirit. Motion says they wanted literature to "seem part of an ordinary hard-drinking, hard-swearing life."

At this time Larkin's Lawrence mania reached its high water mark: he read his favorite daily, like the Bible: "to me, Lawrence is what Shakespeare was to Keats and all the other buggers. . . . As Lawrence says, life is a question of what you thrill to. But there has been a change in the English psyche." Larkin does not expatiate on the change but my point in this book is that a new sensibility was being born, a rough, take-it-or-leave-it honesty and integrity; it was quite different from the aestheticism of the moderns. Lawrence— poet of blood consciousness and the life force—pointed the way: artistically he's miles from the craftsmanship of the moderns; his stories and novels repeat, lecture, hammer and rant, but don't stand as the hard, gem-like icons of Pound and Eliot. This was the directness and distance from art that Larkin responded to.

Larkin's idea of "thrill to" of course included none of Lawrence's bold sexuality. But a problem in *Sons and Lovers* must have spoken to Larkin in a special way: Paul Morel's temperament rebelled against the overwhelming force of sexuality, the power that women had to threaten the artist's identity. Paul feared Miriam Lievers' smothering sensuality—and Larkin was to spend a lifetime dealing with the conflict between his craving for affection and his need for solitude in which to create. How close was too close? Could a woman sap your energy and ruin you? Such sexist speculations were very real to Larkin and were part of his peculiar kind of masculine assertion, nastiness, and cynicism. Being selfish—and being more than a bit proud of it—was part of being a poet.

With two biographies and letters available for public inspection, Larkin's romantic life has become an oddly sensational event in modern English literary history. His passions were not directed at fashionable poetesses, actresses, salonists, high fashion models, or daughters of peers. His girlfriends worked at universities; two had library jobs. The whole thing was so unadventurous that it hit a live nerve with any reader who had grown up dully, fallen into a job and into sexual affairs, longed for pleasure and feared death.

Larkin made the voice in his poems seem like that of Every Brit, not like the swells or the aesthetic elite.

The end of his Oxford career and the beginning of his work life had this unglamorous flavor. Yes, he pulled himself together academically and got a First in the Schools; but the glittering prize that gives a mile-high feeling and very often leads to more and more prizes, great positions, fellowships, and prestige, didn't produce the expected results. Larkin's first job was in a provincial library, not the Foreign Office. In 1943 he accepted a position in the library at Wellington in Shropshire. He thought of himself as not a scholar or technician "but just a nice chap to have around." Such understatement doesn't at all capture his long and distinguished run as a leader and innovator in his field. By the end of his days he was directing a huge operation at the University of Hull—with an enormous budget and building project, not to mention the fact that he received the Queen Mother on an official visit in 1959. But in the mid-1940s he was stumbling into a job, working on a novel about Oxford, and starting his romantic career. Of course there was a war on, but after some anxiousness about being called up, he failed the physical. He missed the big one as he would miss many another experience.

One day a 16-year-old girl named Ruth Bowman came into the library, and from then on Larkin practiced his peculiar rough and tender, mean and caring version of modern love. Chivalry, professions of affection, yearning, and ardor: the words do not apply to Larkin. He was, as Ruth put it, "starving for company" and for sex, but he had no capacity for romance. First of all girls were expensive, time-consuming, and emotionally draining. His crude views separate him from risk-taking moderns like Yeats, Joyce, and Lawrence. "Love collides with selfishness and they're both pretty powerful things."

During his affair with Ruth—an affair that was consummated in 1945—he was under the tutelage of Kingsley Amis, a fellow who believed that girls should pay on dates and not be allowed to dominate one's thoughts. Larkin was an apt pupil, adding his own formulation: it was a shame to treat "without BEING ALLOWED TO SHAG the woman afterwards AS A MATTER OF COURSE."

Now post-adolescent grossness, the awfulness of a twenty-something, is only part of the problem here because Larkin never really outgrew his tendency to be a cad. He was a man who could fascinate with his literary ambition, taste, drive, love of books, and intense artistic experiences, loyalty to friends, but he was in his relations with women (as he commented to his longest running partner, Monica Jones) "no good." This is not to say that he couldn't love, but it all does amount to a self-absorbed, calculating kind of loving. The disease that was his emotional life—a desire to be exalted and intense, but an equal desire to frustrate the development of a relationship—was a major subject of his poetry. In his warped romances, his gloomy look at human happiness, his nasty cracks about sex, he lived the themes of his verse. Yet running through this world of disappointment was also a strong sense of the beautiful and the pleasurable. The struggle to live and experience joy is everywhere in his poems and affairs.

He had plenty of good times with Ruth. She went to the University of London to study, and they met at pubs. They hung around the war ravaged city, took in theater, ate whale steak and other hard-times meals, and enjoyed each other's talk. He confessed that he could open up with her; she would later remember that gentleness and consideration (!) were also mixed in with his self-absorption. They played at being a bear and a cat—which reminds one of John Osborne's bears and squirrels in *Look Back in Anger*. She was shocked and amused by his bawdy language and "outrageous sentiments." He took her to Oxford and showed her "all his favorite places, pubs and beauty spots." One time they went on a literary pilgrimage, "romantically like two Hardy characters trudging from Casterbridge to Bulmouth." It was all very companionable and grittily real. She remembered the road to Hardy country as "flanked by nasty garages and ribbon-developed houses." But after a time the pally quality of their relationship wasn't enough for her. He had produced a ring, but he failed to produce a wedding ceremony. He diagnosed himself in "Wild Oats," a poem where Ruth is depicted as the plain girl "in specs": he was "too selfish, withdrawn / And easily bored to love."

Nevertheless he tried several more times. His affairs with two of the women reveal him in all his blokish awfulness and honesty. After taking a library position at the University of Leicester, he soon met Monica Jones, a striking beauty who taught English and had also gotten an Oxford First. When she saw him at a café she thought him a "snorer," but soon she changed her mind on the basis of his literary talent. So began a long affair, one with a lot of literary companionship and a common understanding of what was witty, unconventional, and ironic. They enjoyed the same things—including vacations at solidly English vacation spots—but their goals were far apart: his were literary achievement and just the right amount of erotic stimulation whereas hers was the happiness of a committed relationship. He was constantly afraid that she might move in with him—which, when years passed and she became ill, was something that came about. But he fought against full-time intimacy, and during their 14-year relationship he took up with another woman, Maeve Brennan. He was working at the University of Hull by this time, and Maeve was "a superior dogsbody," far from the level of the top-flight academic Monica. Larkin tutored her for the Library Association exam and mixed funny business and business. She was a Roman Catholic and it took some time to wear down her resistance about sex, but she gave in and they were on and off as lovers for years. He thought of her—this, an uncharacteristic romantic touch—as Yeats's Maude Gonne. She was nothing of the kind; unlike the statuesque, commanding woman who drove Yeats to poetry, Maeve was lively, sociable and accessible, and possessed of an everyday shrewdness. She summed up Larkin's nature with great accuracy: "A man of remarkable talent, he loved the commonplace."

The predictable things emerged from his relationships with these two women: discovery of the other, rancor, jealousy, guilt (on his part), rage (on theirs). Monica's tone is perfectly fitted to the whole mess: "He lied to me, the bugger, but I loved him." Larkin received letters from Maeve while on holiday with Monica—and told the latter that he was "so careless of your feelings and so bloody bad-mannered, even." He knew about the behavior of a gentleman, but he had no intention of making it a reality. In 1978 the University of Hull honored him with a performance of *Larkinland*, a dramatic presentation of his work. He wouldn't take Maeve to the reception. Andrew Motion speaks of his lack of remorse, but there's also a certain positive quality here, an honest admission of what he was. "I'm *not* a philanderer, I'm *not* accustomed to keeping lots of girls on a string, I'm extremely faithful by nature. The trouble is there are lots of less laudable characteristics in me as well, I suppose." The "I suppose" is the what-do-you-want-from-me cri de coeur of the bloke: take me as I am; I have no code; I live as I must, torn between pleasure and pain.

Larkin completed his romantic career by having a third affair—this time with a very matronly looking librarian named Betty Mackereth. She was his strong right arm at work and the one who performed the grim task of destroying his diary when he was near the end, dying of cancer. The pages were not meant for our eyes, and Betty, unlike Kafka's friend Max Brod, didn't give us a chance to see more of a tormented and frustrated man whose art is intertwined with his personality. It's all very well to separate the man who suffers and the artist who creates, to observe the niceties of "persona" vs. real man, to avoid flat-footed identifications of characters with their authors. But biography—with its places and events and moods and characters—does illuminate the nature of an imaginative work, if not its value. The reader of

Larkin does well to know his temperament and his opinions, his Coventry and Hull.

Larkin's poetry broke with the emotional flights and adventures in language of the last two hundred years. He dispensed with the self-celebration and up-in-the-air philosophizing of the romantics; he wanted nothing to do with the avant-garde edge, fragmentation, symbolism, and pyrotechnics of the modernists. Instead he created a direct, idiomatic kind of verse that cut to the heart of everyone's quotidian existence. Vague longing, disappointment, dispiriting atmosphere, frustration, disgust, and fear of death: these were the themes that he thrust upon readers with his characteristic blunt wit. "Deprivation is for me what daffodils were for Wordsworth," he once commented.

The critic Christopher Carduff points out that "Larkinism" is "a private label poetic shtick." By this he means there's something a bit annoying about the pose of the nay-sayer, loser, plodder, doleful victim of fate. (Motion has compared Larkin to Eyore.) Larkin, after all, won tremendous recognition for a small body of work, enjoyed such honors as an honorary degree from Oxford, went to Buckingham Palace for his CBE (with Monica). Yet in "Party Politics" he writes, "I never remember holding a full drink." Complaint, regret, and loss are everywhere in the work. The ardor and expansiveness of the romantics, the glamorous contemplation of the abyss which characterized the moderns should be contrasted with Larkin's hard and steady look at the diminishment all around us. Larkin refused to soar, play the bard, or strike anything but a jarring, unfashionable pose. He wrote two novels—*Jill* and *Girl in Winter*—but for all their skill, they are both dreamy accounts of ineffectual lives minus the bite and wit of Larkin's best poetic language. He made a false start in poetry with *North Ship*, a book with a lot of abstract language and vaporous emotion. But the real artist emerged in the 1950s in *The Less Deceived*. The poems were rhymed and metered to give pleasure, but otherwise as direct as prose statements. Larkin's persona never changed—he was alive, honest, keenly aware of human suffering. He wrote about three basic things: his battered Britain, his letdowns, and his rage.

Take one of his most famous poems, "Church Going." A clueless modern Brit enters a church, removes his "cycle-clips in awkward reverence," walks around, and encounters a thousand years of Christendom. While inspecting a spiritual place that has never meant anything to him, he achieves his own recognition. Larkin makes his clumsiness and vague boredom ways of understanding. And there's something ironically humorous about the ignorance and insensitivity. As the tourist lets the door "thud shut" (all bluntness intended), we laugh at "there's nothing going on" and the weary phrase "Another church." The "holy end" and the "unignorable silence, / Brewed God knows how long" are rude and uncomprehending, but the language wakes us up. Plain blokespeak leads somewhere important: in wondering what to look for, he discovers his own spiritual sense. What is to come when belief is ended, superstition has come and gone, and even disbelief has grown old? He has "no idea / What this accoutred frowsty barn is worth" yet he is strangely pleased to be in it. Larkin's honest doubter—someone who refers to the believer as a "Christmas addict" or "ruin bibber"—is busy doubting himself. For someone "bored, uninformed," he's very interested: the "silence" which existed for God knows how long gives pleasure. With an awkward, groping vocabulary, he blurts out his recognition: the church is a place where "someone will forever be surprising / A hunger in himself to be more serious." The wonderful alliteration makes the line epigrammatic, a piece of spiritual wisdom. It should also be said that the poem has traveled the distance from flippancy to seriousness. But without the blokish language (including church going, like movie going), the poem would be a dry meditation.

A variety of other private and public spaces also let Larkin be his characteristic lonely and diminished self. The poems often lack the affirmation of "Church Going" and instead leave us with bleak enlightenment. In "Mr. Bleaney" the speaker occupies a room once inhabited by an old man. He learns Bleaney's tastes, habits, and routines—and we begin to think he may become a Bleaney himself. With its worn curtain and view of a "tussocked, littered" bit of land, the room has all the right equipment for a desperate life, including a "saucer-souvenir" to stub fags in. The speaker says he doesn't know whether Bleaney shook "off the dread / That how we live measures our own nature." Not knowing—it would seem—is a sure way of knowing: it's like Larkin's "I suppose," a resigned way of saying one is overwhelmed by truth. There's also plenty of irony and sadness in "I'll take it": the Larkin persona accepts his fate.

There are two other important poems that use a room with a Larkin view—"High Windows" and "Aubade." The first is a strange blend of everyday crudity and metaphysical awareness. Whenever the speaker of the poem sees "a couple of kids" and guesses "he's fucking her and she's taking pills or wearing a diaphragm," he moves into a fantasy of fulfillment. This very English poem (with phrases such as "an outdated combine harvester," "bloody birds," and "hell and that") is about what "Everyone old has dreamed of all their lives"—unfettered freedom, frustration-free Englishness. But the high window looks out on "Nothing," and that nothing is "endless." The infinite in Larkin is bleaker than the prospect of a littered building lot. The room described in "Aubade," an uncollected poem, is another place of fear, this time the very definite fear of death. Nothing is now described as "Not to be here, / Not to be anywhere, / And soon: Nothing more terrible, nothing more true." As the persona wakes at four in the morning, he describes "curtain edges" growing "light." "Unresting death" is already awake—such is Larkin's grim humor. Larkin's terrifying plainness is everywhere—in the physical details of very early morning ("telephones crouch" or "the uncaring / Intricate rented world begins to rouse") and in the rhetoric ("Being brave / Lets no one off the grave").

Let's go outside, to Larkin's landscapes. Numbers of poems look at the ravaged, weary country that a poet with no sentimental side took as his own. Some of the best of these pieces are "I Remember, I Remember," "Going, Going," "Here," "Essential Beauty," and "Sunny Penstatyn." These explorations of locale are one of the most solid parts of Larkin's achievement. In English poetry they have a place alongside Blake's "London," which is to say they make topography vibrate with feelings and ideas.

The earliest of these verses is "I Remember, I Remember," published in 1954, the year of "Church Going." It too is a look at England's past, but at literary and social traditions rather than religion. Larkin provides images from an idyllic childhood and adolescence, references to the formative years of poets: the scene for all this is Coventry, his birth place. Yet these pieces of English memory are gathered together for the purpose of reminding us that they were never part of the speaker's life. That cozy poetic England—that tight little island of *Country Life*, old photo albums, popular fiction—has a garden where a poet-in-the-making would have invented "Blinding theologies of flowers and fruits." It has the young creator spoken to "by an old hat"—and of course it has well-built boys and "girls all chest," as well as romantic episodes "Where she / Lay back." To top it off, this England has the wonderful story of a poet's first publications and his early recognition. The only trouble is that the story is pure fantasy. The town is where "my childhood was unspent," where nothing happened. The speaker in the poem has a traveling companion who says, "You look as if you wished the place in hell." Nothing of the sort: "I suppose it's not the place's fault." Again, the Larkin "I suppose" to register pain and resignation. Even memory of place—that precious English commodity from Gray's Stoke Poges to Wordsworth's Tintern Abbey to Eliot's Little Gidding—has been diminished. But the lack of romantic or spiritual charge makes the poet work double time; he supplies his uniquely disillusioned attitude to fill the gap.

"Going, Going," a late poem, is a different, more devastating story. The problem is not the dullness of the Coventry middle-class neighborhood, but the expunging of all social character. The nation is fast becoming just another place where "more houses, more parking [are] allowed." "[T]he Tourist parts" will endure, but the rest will become "the first slum of Europe"—and Larkin rhymes "parts" with "the crooks and tarts" who will take over. The place will become a developer's venture—mostly "concrete and tyres," with no meadows or guildhalls or other things that are not bankable assets. This blunt vision is made artful and moving by Larkin's injection of his own sad self—"before I snuff it" and "I just think it will happen" being two phrases that show the poet's prosaic language doing its best work.

"Here," a more elusive and suggestive poem than the last two, is about coming into the city of Hull from the countryside, taking in the commercial district, and leaving. It's not a pretty tour, and the poet makes it uncomfortable from the start by repeating the word "swerving." The "surprise of a large town" after "solitude / Of skies and scarecrows" is no delight either. We follow "residents from raw estates" as they are "brought down" (surely a pun) by "flat-faced trolleys" to the shopping area. People "push through swing doors to their desires," including "cheap suits" and "iced lollies." They are "a cut price crowd," writes nasty Larkin; they stay among their relatives or hang out with salespeople in the stores. Larkin distinguishes them from the residents of Hull who live down in the "fish smelling" section near the slave museum (neither image conducive to a pleasant visit). Larkin moves out of town before long, observing the "mortgaged half-built edges." Soon we are in the country again, but its "unfenced existence" is "untalkative, out of reach." This mysterious, bleak ending is a good deal like the one in "High Windows." It's metaphysical no man's land, where Larkin meets the terrors of absence.

But Larkinland is also filled with plenty of amusing flaws, notably on display in "Sunny Penstatyn" and "Essential Beauty." His mischievous eye and playful sense of the bawdy are conspicuous in the first—not that either blots out his grim realism. Penstatyn is advertised on a billboard featuring a laughing girl in "tautened white satin." There's "a hunk of coast" (Larkin the deflator at work) and a hotel which "seemed to expand from her thighs." This image of happy post-World War II Britain—a nation trying to have its bit of holiday fun—is grotesquely defaced. The big picture of a pretty girl is given "huge tits" and "a fissured crotch" by someone named "Titch Thomas." It's as if the poster has become a huge, gross, horrible parody of the century old naughty seaside postcard. For those who don't recall, such cards depicted humorous scenes of bodacious girls, overweight tourists, and the rough and tumble amusements of working-class people on hol. George Orwell's "The Art of Donald Magill" deals with one of the masters of such ribaldry; the crude jokes and cheesy images are a particular form of British social release—being on holiday from politeness and respectability, really. Larkin shows us that, if truth be told, sex and bawdiness can be creepy; his compassionate side is repelled by the fact that someone tore through her defaced lips. The poor girl "was too good for this life." Readers inclined to write Larkin off as an old cynic should instead consider his respect and deep feeling for British femininity: the girl in the poster is like the girls and women in *Peg's Paper*, a working-class women's magazine. Richard Hoggart in his pioneering book *The Uses of Literacy* described the ways in which such decent women and their values "speak for a solid and relevant way of life." Despite their garish tastes and their sentimentality, they want stability, a home, and the nicer things. The only trouble, according to Larkin, is the nastiness and despair that have won the day. In place of the girl, there will be another billboard—"Fight Cancer." Larkin manages to create a disturbing assonance with "tear," "hand," "Cancer," "there."

"Essential Beauty" is also about billboard Britain, this time a nation where ads "dominate out doors." The poem, written in

1962, could serve as a good illustration of French philosopher Baudrillard's "simulacra" theory. Images and illusions overwhelm the real—"great loaves" of bread block streets, "custard" screens graveyards, and "cuts of salmon" and fuel oil cover slums. Larkin, the poet of clever rhymes, who loves song lyrics, begins with "In frames as large as rooms." Larkin, the sardonic observer, says Britishers look to these images for some "essential beauty" in their all-too-real world of "rained on streets." Yearning for the ideal, they are most often frustrated. A boy, sick in the Gents, "just missed" the pub poster of "white clothed ones from tennis-clubs"; and Larkin goes over the top by saying that an old man wanted to taste pure, unadulterated old age and therefore paid an extra half-penny for "Granny Graveclothes Tea." We end with "dying smokers" trying to make out the image of a glamorous woman on a billboard: no amount of lighting up and dragging on a cigarette ever "brought" her "near"—in real life, that is. But in billboard life she's "clear": "smiling, recognizing, and going dark." Larkin's disillusionment extends to all the Truth and Beauty that's sold in public.

Larkin's temperament didn't require a thoroughly realized locale to express itself. Like Blake or Yeats, he could spin out complex feelings, aspects of his personality, and universal yearnings from a set theme. Blake did this in "Mock on, Mock on," Yeats in many poems including "The Choice" and "The Fascination of What's Difficult." Larkin's reflections on work, money, death, sex, and love are in the tradition of such poetic didacticism. They're brilliantly crafted messages about eternal questions. "Toads" and "Toads Revisited" concern the curse/blessing of work, a subject that Yeats treated in "Adam's Curse." Larkin the deglamorizer makes the labor in question the drudgery of the daily worker rather than the hard-won triumph of the poet. His tone is that of the average man complaining and pointing to "them"—the fortunate slackers. He cries out against his own unwillingness to drive off the toad of work which "squat[s] on my life." This rant is couched in strangely clever diction that blends the contemporary and the quaintly archaic. (All that time put in on Anglo-Saxon at Oxford counted for something.) *Stuff your pension!* and "paying a few bills" alternate with "losels" and "loblolly-men" (scoundrels and odd-job fellows). Larkin's speaker fumes with the resentment of the ages; the antique, worn-out diction (including "paupers" and "folk" "who live up lanes" and their "nippers" and "whippet-thin wives") makes us realize that Larkin is railing against the burden of civilization. Dreams of liberation are no match for the inner toad in him, the demanding superego which "hunkers as heavy as hard luck." He can't bluff his way to fulfillment because the pleasure principle and the reality principle battle it out in his life and make him the neurotic he is: others are of course no better off, but the irritated narrator takes civilization personally.

He gets even grimmer when he accepts his fate in "Toads Revisited." The poem looks at working and slacking and gives the edge to the former. This second try at the theme has a richer emotional flavor. It also adds liberal measures of English scenery, even though the look of things is not the point. This material makes didacticism come alive. A walk in the park should "feel better than work," but it doesn't. Then the speaker proceeds, in an often nasty way, to depict those who have time for parks, including "palsied old step-takers" and "characters in long coats." Larkin, the famous (or infamous) admirer of Mrs. Thatcher, here makes exceptionally fine verse out of Tory rhetoric: the unemployed dodge work because they're "stupid or weak." They examine "their failures" beside "beds of lobelias." Larkin doesn't reserve the biting, sarcastic rhymes for losers, however; the up-and-doing like himself have their "in-tray" and their "loaf-haired secretary," hardly images of the satisfactions of work and success. And this is what keeps this lyric about being busy from being obnoxious: it's a totally honest piece about "old toad" helping the speaker "down Cemetery Road." No political booster could ever quite like Larkin's brutal take on industriousness.

And no businessman would ever care for what Larkin writes in "Money." The poem is a brilliantly depressing reflection on cash and quality of life, but wealth management specialists will no sooner brighten up when they hear "a second house and car and wife" than they will cringe at "you can't put off being young until you retire." Larkin concludes by looking out one of his famous windows with a view on the unadorned truth. He hears "money singing" and then moves to an epic simile of "looking down" on "a provincial town": it's the same dismal scene we know from the landscape poems. "It is intensely sad." The song of money began as a sharp reproach: why don't you spend your way into "goods and sex," with "a few cheques"; it ended with a line that slows to a deathly pace—one that has a period in the middle.

Sex and love are the respective themes of "Annus Mirabilis" and "An Arundel Tomb": both poems show Larkin working coolly with passionate material. He avoids what the bloke Hazlitt railed against—cant. Convictions and feelings are never run into the ground; they're never allowed to run at all. Instead we get a rueful, sly Larkin persona making very familiar subject matter sound odd. The brisk jog-trot rhythms of the first piece clash violently with the depressing situation, which is nothing less than a brief history of modern sexuality: old style repression from the 1940s and 1950s, new style liberation which started in 1963. (Larkin the cultural chronicler enjoys echoing, in his tart way, the line of Virginia Woolf about modernity beginning in 1910.) Both old and new sex are given a bitter spin. The old was "bargaining / A wrangle for a ring"—a quarrel, really, about economics. But the new style is also depicted as "breaking the bank"—"an unlosable game." Both are about advantage gained. Meanwhile, the poet lost both games—"nineteen sixty-three" was "just too late for me" and, be it remembered, he was "part of a shame," all the prudery, in his youth. The period between the lifting of the *Chatterley* ban and "the Beatles first LP" is the beginning of something good, but you wouldn't know it from the tone of this poem. "So life was never better" sounds fairly sour.

There's plenty of backing off from joy, love, and fulfillment in "An Arundel Tomb." The poem is a curious affirmation built on negations, false assumptions, and plain untruths. Larkin's I-suppose mode is here raised to a high power as he is forced to see love in an effigy that probably only came to be as a mark of social importance. The tomb has two medieval figures—an earl and countess—who are presented without any of the dreamy style of a poet contemplating the romantic past: Larkin's Middle Ages emerge in the dry, crisp language of an author who knows nothing of charm or enchantment. The speaker is about to show you the unadorned truth: "blurred" faces and "stiffened pleat" do not invite awe or admiration; the little dog at the couple's feet has the "hint of the absurd." No sooner does the poet get a "tender shock" from the earl's hand holding hers than he pulls back and reminds us (in almost condescending language) that it's "a sculptor's sweet commissioned grace"—a medieval publicity stunt to make the effigy memorable. The couple most probably had no tender feelings—their "supine stationary voyage" is Larkin's hard, clear image of the past coming into our time; the two are "helpless in the hollow / Of an unarmorial age," a mere "scrap of history." When he says that "an attitude remains" he means the "stone fidelity" that they "hardly meant" (the pun of "hard" is intended) is transfigured over time: only love remains, which is to say that future generations, ironically, will understand the hand clasp not the hard reality of long ago. We the beholders will get a wrong, but beautiful message. Larkin's natural cynicism and perversity here serve an odd and tender purpose.

Two masterful poems about time and loss, "At Grass" and "Show Saturday," strike an elegiac note but do so in Larkin's matter-of-fact way. Characteristically, Larkin draws an effect from the opposite effect: in this case diminishment from the fullness of life. "At Grass" is about thoroughbred race horses and the cups and

stakes of 15 years ago. Winning and fame are here rendered pow-
erless by time. Larkin's images of these steeds out to pasture are
subtly dispiriting: a shade makes the horses all but invisible; wind
distresses tail and mane; anonymity is conveyed by words like
"faint afternoons," "faded, classic Junes," "stole away." The once
famous horses "have slipped their names"; field glasses and stop
watches no longer keep track of them. Larkin makes the assonance
of "groom" and "evening come" work beautifully in the last two
lines.

"Show Saturday," a much longer and even more complex piece,
deals with a sense of loss coming out of a sense of busyness and
energy. This time it's not champions but bustling country people
who fade out. Dogs and ponies and sheep and balloon men and
acrobats and produce and arts and crafts of every sort make the
poem an incredibly rich genre painting, somewhat like a Victorian
canvas capturing the plenitude of social life, its types and occupations. "It's the ended husk of summer," and Larkin takes stock of
British enterprise: he inventories everything from eggs to needle-
work in a loving portrait; it's "all worthy, all well done." This is
the moral center of Larkin's world: "Let it always be there." But
the drift of the poem—apparent by midpoint—is about the end
of things. "Back now" is a refrain—and the show "dies back."
Larkin calls it—in his throwaway manner—"something people
do": it's a force that emerges "ancestrally each year." People don't
realize that time "shadows" greater deeds. At once celebratory and
doleful, the poem is Larkin at his most balanced.

But numbers of other fine poems in his volumes are notable
for their extremism: they rant and ventilate and proudly sport
rudeness and crudity. Larkin, more than any post-World War II
British poet, pioneered the dictional revolution, made vulgarity and obscenity the thing of the future. Unlike Wordsworth,
Larkin wrote no preface to *High Windows*; yet this work—and
to some extent *Whitsun Weddings*—contains a powerful change
in the nature of the poet's voice. From here on a poet could be a

bloke speaking to blokes; a poem could be a spontaneous overflow of nasty feelings recollected with irony and irritation.

Although the late seventeenth and early eighteenth century was not much on Larkin's mind, he shared a lot with Dryden and Swift when it comes to scatological insult and witty abusiveness. Dryden's *MacFlecknoe* ranks out its subject, the poet Shadwell, and likens him to excrement; Swift's imagination in *Gulliver's Travels* and in numbers of poems is excremental. Larkin's "Vers de Société" begins, "My wife and I have asked a crowd of craps / To come and waste their time and ours: perhaps." The answer: "In a pig's arse." The poem then proceeds to heap abuse on nice chaps and ladies for no apparent reason, except if you count the vague reason that they are intellectual nullities. This obnoxious charge takes us back to Dryden and Swift (and Pope, of course), those poets of reason and good sense and wit. But Larkin, in characteristic fashion, intends to exchange one emotion for another, in this case rage at the ordinary for need of companionship. Yes, society involves waste of time, "drivel," "holding a glass of washing sherry," "forks and faces"—and no solid payoff. Larkin goes further by saying that "having people nice to you" is what our civilization is all about; "playing at goodness" is our form of "going to church." Yet social life bores us, and we're bad at it. "(Asking that ass about his fool research)" Larkin then reaches for the truth behind the social charade. Social life is scoffable on the whole, but it does keep us from thinking of other things. He names two— "failure and remorse." In his clever and mordant way he has gone from mocking the emptiness of a social gathering to exposing the emptiness of the self.

Larkin's poetry of insult in the main is directed at the yawning gap where meaning should be—he rages against the hollow lives of people alone and people in groups. He doesn't care whom he hurts—even himself. "The life with a Hole in it" is an uncollected piece written in the early 1970s; its title says a lot and its nasty diction combines with its social sweep to make it a small triumph—of disappointment, that is. First we have Larkin howling (as he did as a teenager) about not getting the quality of life he wants; then we have an "old ratbags" who says he's always had his own way. Larkin's answer? Well, "the shit in the shuttered chateau" who writes a bit and plays around for the rest of the day has one possible way of life—that's out; and then again, the "school-teaching sod" with six kids "and the wife in pod" is also someone he can't be. "The unbeatable slow machine" of life brings "what you'll get." The only thing that comes out of this is that time passes and we realize what limited creatures we are. The same theme dominates "Self's the Man," an early poem that's snide about other lives, but also spares the narrator nothing. Someone named Arnold with a wife and kiddies is probably less selfish than the persona; he's the kind of fellow who lets domesticity engulf him, who willingly writes letters to his mother-in-law to come for the summer. Yet maybe Arnold likes his fate; and perhaps the only difference between two selfish men is that the poet has more self knowledge about what he can endure. Larkin's "I suppose" occurs in the last line—which is to say we see him at a pitch of self-absorption, worrying about whether he's selfish.

That's at least something when you compare it to the fate of the very elderly, the subjects of "The Old Fools." The first few lines are a devastating attack on loss of consciousness; Larkin mocks senility and wonders why the old aren't screaming about their losses. Larkin's Strulbrugs, the poet speculates, probably think they're somewhere else, somewhere in the past: actually they're at the foot of "Extinction's alp," not knowing what's in front of them. And most people, according to Larkin's "This Be the Verse," don't know that loss and pain are unintended consequences of living; your mum and dad "fuck you up," without meaning to; they give you their faults, like grim gifts, and add "some extra, just for you." Larkin's message—population zero as the cure—is sour and simplistic, but the poem's strange blend of the vulgar and the mysterious works. Human unhappiness is like a "coastal shelf," getting gradually deeper. Larkin's mordant look at the end of Empire is also a poem about not knowing what the loss means: it's hard to know, the poet says, if someone caused it, if it makes a difference. Maybe it's better to have the money to bequeath to a new generation. Our children will probably not even know that Britain is a different country.

In any event, Larkin has told the story of his time, place, and sensibility with the unsparing honesty and arresting technique of a new writer. He dared to be frank and forthright, to ignore the entertainment value of avant-garde presentation, and to tell his truths in trenchant verse.

3

KINGSLEY AMIS

"Does he drink? Is he jolly?" Kingsley Amis asked about a young man who was coming to visit him from the States. The questions go to the heart of Amis's personality and the literary personae that he created. Kingsley's world smells of beer and malt scotch and is relentlessly convivial, even when all kinds of nasty emotions enter it. He is the first famous literary bloke of the post-World War II period, the writer who made risk, edginess, rudeness, transgression, boredom-busting, subversion, mischief, and Schadenfreude his lifetime occupations. He worked at these things full-time for five decades, cultivating an image and creating a type that endured. But the making of that image was well under way by the early 1960s—and it is with the earlier years up through the beginning of the international counterculture that we are concerned. Amis was a man whose nature was formed before writers and average people had heard anything of the New Left, student protests, alternate lifestyles, and all the other trappings of the counterculture. His brand of subversion was something older, a contrarian's naysaying, sneering and mockery directed at the sham and stuffiness of British culture. In the 1940s when he was a student at Oxford—and much later when he truculently defended Thatcherism—it had a political element, but that was never really the point. The battle that he waged in his books and in everyday life was really about manly integrity not public policy. "The manly man stubbornly insists upon himself," philosopher Harvey Mansfield writes. This is the Amis project: assertion—humorous, cutting, hurtful—in a world where all the odds seem to be against the manly self.

In *Look Back in Anger* John Osborne's protagonist Jimmy Porter, a young man in the 1950s, cries out that there are no more brave causes. Amis actually beat Osborne to the insight. Several years before Jimmy proclaimed the stifling of spirit and the dreary reign of middle class apathy, Amis was on the job in *Lucky Jim*, his landmark book about one lively Englishman's battle with social and cultural tedium. And that book came from a young writer who had thought about the unvital elements in his culture since adolescence, his *Memoirs* are a steady recollection of bland surroundings, snobbishness, dead-end careers, dullness and desperation trying to seem like sprightliness and hope. His life as a writer was one long and often quite funny attempt to break away from all the pain-producing things that he was so used to. Harvey Mansfied says that the manly man has to risk a great deal in order to save his life from insignificance; in the course of living with *thumos*, spiritedness to the ancient Greeks, a man can get involved with uncontrolled aggression, brutality, and every kind of irrationality. But the object of the good life for the risk takers is pleasure, joy, the sense that one's own being is not to be swept aside. Kingsley Amis had a lifelong anxiety, which he expressed quite plainly: the fear that the "BORING CRAPS" would win the day. Overcoming this fear became a career.

His life began in Norbury, S.W. 16, a ward of the London borough of Croydon, as nondescript a locale as it's possible to imagine. Neither prosperous nor poor, urban nor rural, it was "not a place" in the sense of a spot with any past or reason for being other than as an opportunity for developers. On the railroad line to London, it was a station around which shops and housing sprouted up. "No rubbish about roots for Norbury," Amis remarks. The sketch of the houses in Zachary Leader's biography of Amis looks like a Platonic idea of a suburb—small single family houses and trees. Amis bluntly states his point about such non-places and their inhabitants: there's no "glamour potential" in the "urban or suburban middle classes." Like university degrees, extremes are interesting: a First or a Fourth, several bathrooms in a house or none. Amis, untrue to the English love of understatement, seemed to thrive on over-the-top effects in writing and living. Bluntness is part of his game, in every aspect of life—his family, for example. There's nothing roundabout or sly in the depiction of grandparents. His maternal grandfather, a prosperous glassworks owner, is described as having a mottled nose, long hairs emerging therefrom, a capacity to laugh but not smile, a tendency to tell funny stories, and a settled indifference to his grandson. Amis puts his reaction this way: "I have only realized since preparing to write this how much I disliked and was repelled by him." The paternal grandmother, Mater, was "a large, dreadful, hairy-faced creature," controlling in the extreme, who had her glasses of port brought out from the pub to her car. On the mother's side there was Grandad, a man who liked to collect "real books"; he was the only grandparent Amis liked. His wife, Gran, was likened to "one of those horrible shrunken little old women dressed in black who used to sit on the walls or outside shops on the Continent." She lived in Camberwell, "the archetype of the place the hero in the rags-to-riches film swears at the age of ten to be a thousand miles way from." Gran's conversation ran to such topics as "Lily's cough was worse and Nell could not have long to go now." George Orwell covered this spirit-numbing lower-middle-class ethos in *Keep the Aspidistra Flying*: all the whining, life-denying, peevish, mean strategies of people who were a bit above the working class. Amis specialized in finding every mutation of such deadness—from the narrowness of his own set to every kind of narrowness in higher places. General British awfulness was his theme, something he captured with relish.

His own father appears to have been less awful than his grandparents, but also to have marks of woe that made him rather pathetic. William was not an ignorant man, having been to the famous City of London School, that democratic nursery of men of achievement located for years on the Victoria Embankment. But his occupational destiny was no larger than a decent paying position at Coleman's Mustard. Amis called him "the most English human being I have ever known." Given what he describes in the man's character, this is not a compliment. William, like his father, was jokey and self-absorbed. He liked mimicry, comic imitations of business associates and foreigners and deaf people, storytelling, cricket, and complaining about the pushiness of people nowadays. As a boy Amis was introduced to his father's favorites in music, Gilbert and Sullivan. (He turned to Brahms and jazz.) As a young man he complained of "my male relative": Daddy A, as he came to be known, was bumptious and intrusive, talked to Amis's friends, tried to impress with his wit and was generally a bore. Having left the religious world of chapel and joined the Church of England, he adopted a kind of moralism and censoriousness—especially about sexual matters—without having any real faith.

While Kinsley Amis kept the social side of Daddy A's ridiculousness out of his memoirs, they are important for an understanding of the novelist's sense of absurdity. In matters of class, William was most English. He had the age-old obsession with deference, one's place in society, appropriate behavior, tasteful gentility and suspicion of "them"—new people with more money. For better or worse, Daddy A was part of his son's life until he died. He went to America with Amis when the famous author of *Lucky Jim* was on his way to teach creative writing at Princeton. Onboard ship he was out of his depth with well-traveled and well-bred people. In Washington, DC, visiting his sister, he tried to get invited as a British subject to a reception for the Queen. He received a polite turndown. Things were better in terms of acceptance on the voyage home. He booked first class and enjoyed cocktails with the

Purser. Daddy A apparently wrote an 11,000 word manuscript about his American journey, detailing the rebuffs, the cheekiness of black porters in DC, and the fun of being accepted. Amis let a friend see the manuscript but was himself unwilling to keep it.

The household Amis grew up in was carefully managed by his mother Peggy, a mousy, giggly, fairly attractive woman. She overprotected and overfed her only child and Amis's biographer Zachary Leader hazards the guess that the future novelist was driven by a strong desire to break out of the confines of home. The place had plenty of chintz, porcelain figurines, and "bunny rabbit ornaments." Amis does seem to relish the story of his aunt Dora, someone who did—in a sorry way—break out of the dreariness of her class. An obsessive compulsive who feared already extinguished matches, Dora wound up in an asylum. But her managerial skills as a caterer made her a great asset to the institution and after her treatment she was given a good job. Amis—in his characteristic brutal fun-loving mode—comments that upon graduation from the place she was given a fellowship. Such nastiness is a part of the bloke's psychic equipment; we will see it time after time as our subjects attempt to cut loose from the awfulness of life. It's as if Amis and others are figuring out a way to go awfulness one better.

Like his father, Amis attended the City of London School, beginning in 1934. He started his career, strangely enough, as a joker and mimic—just the things he would ridicule about the old man. The school determined a boy's acceptance by his amiability—not his social credentials—and his popularity by his ability to raise an occasional laugh. Amis scored on both counts and also became a "greyhound" (read quick study) rather than a "dud." His quickness also included a keen eye for the masters' eccentricities and defects; without assigning great insights to himself, Amis says that young boys feel "the delighted, faintly hostile astonishment of the tourist" when they look at grownups. Novelists must know how to "recapture" this fresh contempt, this "coldly wondering stare" of the teenager. Amis was off to a good start as he observed Mr. Ellingham, a classics master who taught well, introduced the boys to landmarks of art and music, played cricket, but was no Mr. Chips. Amis believed Ellingham considered him a greyhound, but he also thought that the master "saw though my affectations." Meanwhile the young boy developed a kind of respect for the teacher that was without warmth: "I have sometimes suspected that Mr. Ellingham did not greatly care for me" is not a line that suggests any intensity on the pupil's part either. Amis knows the worth of the man, but the "coldly wondering stare" persists. The entire school experience is suffused with unnostalgic and unromantic feeling; the roughness of adolescence and the sensitivity to music and literature mix strangely—brutal chumminess, Borodin and Rimsky-Korsakov and Fats Waller, French verse, and contempt for authority. Amis was pals with a Jewish kid named Cyril Metliss, born in his father's pub in Smithfield, who loved music and poetry. According to Leader, he had his first pint in the father's establishment. He also enjoyed the company of one Wybrow, "that great rampager and iconoclast, loping through the cloisters with one hand ready to dart out in assault, the other clutched inward for defence, his whole being permanently gathered for the delivery of a jeering gaffaw, his ravaged face and elbowing, shoving demeanour an advertisement of instinctive revolt."

Amis spent the later part of his school days at Marlborough College, a place of refuge in 1939 for the City of London School. "The unlooked-for descent of five or six hundred dayboys, many of them noisy and tatterdemalion" was nothing that the young gentlemen of Marlborough particularly welcomed. Amis got to eat in the school dining hall, but he also wound up working as a waiter. He only wished Wybrow were still on hand for purposes of "ranging contumeliously across the front court of the college, kicking a Marlborough prefect's rolled umbrella out of his hand or jostling an important parent at the gate." In the *Memoirs* he is "saddened" by the fact that Wybrow disappeared into commerce rather than using his "pulsating violence" to juice up the Sunday papers. He was "his own man," Amis says. (Harvey Mansfield would certainly identify his spirited assertiveness.) Yet a young man of Amis's temperament was unlikely not to find numbers of kindred spirits and to make common cause and wildness with them. He was also going to invent many of them as a writer.

His Oxford days began with a blokish arrival and a grand drunk. He "went up" in 1941 in "impeccably proletarian style," driven by the family butcher in a battered Morris, even going up Plough Lane the wrong way. The opening paragraphs describing the university in his *Memoirs* are a masterful depiction of everything unglamorous. He'd received a "cut-price" scholarship to St John's; he was "allotted a nasty like pair of rooms" since he didn't come from a great public school; he was unused to spirits or wine and got drunk at the sherry party that his school friends at College threw for him; he was found dazed with a chamber-pot in his lap by a contingent of men from the Conservative Association.

The business of being anti-academic got underway immediately. Like his soon-to-be friend Philip Larkin, Amis hated the curriculum and the decorum. The two uncomfortable, rather snarky undergraduates at St John's met in 1941 through a mutual out-of-step friend Norman Iles. Iles, the lower class youth whom we heard about in connection with Larkin, was an "ideal bad undergraduate," a cutter of lectures, and terrific lover of violent humor. One day he and Larkin were together and Iles spotted Amis. "He shoots guns," Iles said. With that Iles pointed a "pistol" finger at Amis and the latter went through a movie scene of throwing his arm up against an archway and tottering forward. Larkin knew his man, which is to say his kindred spirit, from this bit of acting out. "For the first time I felt myself in the presence of a talent greater than my own," Larkin recorded. A talent for what? Disturbance, parody, absurdity, comic letting off steam? The two young men became fast friends. They drank, railed against Oxford, engaged in campy banter, disrespected whatever curricular requirement presented itself. Their assault on the literary canon was described—as it applies to the great works of early centuries—in the last chapter. Amis was the better of the two in this. His period at the University was broken by army service from 1942–45, but there was no break in his contempt for the big texts in English literature that were the bedrock of the curriculum. After the war he had to do some studying—a lot really—but the nasty tone in his voice is clear. "Barewolf" was a "HEAP OF GANGRENED ELEPHANT'S SPUTUM." Dryden was an awful writer to gauge other awful writers by: a full 1 was a Dryden—Keats got .5, Milton .9. Amis the memoirist says that even hearing Chaucer's death date produces "a strong whiff of the depression the thing itself regularly brought me." While irritated and disappointed in the lack of pleasure available in study, Amis was never weak-willed and therefore managed to endure English Literature, go for a First, apply himself—and get that great distinction. Meanwhile, he liked what he liked in reading and general culture, and the only pattern in his tastes seems to be a settled dislike of the self-consciously fabricated, the artificial, the experimental. He hated "shags like Pickarso" and talk of "the blue period," didn't care for Lawrence and all the rhetoric and poetry about sexual instinct. (In this, of course, he differed from Larkin.) But he did read a great deal of twentieth-century literature, using Larkin as his guide. Powell, Auden, and Isherwood, the misogynistic Montherlant, the wacky Irish parodist Flann O'Brien—the latter specialized in making fun of the Celtic temperament and the mistiness of Irish myth. Amis, it should be noted, had a similar nose for the pretensions and excesses of contemporary Englishness.

He was also part of two groups at Oxford that were contrarian and critical of the national pieties. One was the Oxford University Labour Club and the other was a clique called "The Seven." William Amis had been a Lloyd George Liberal and later a staunch

Conservative—both middle class things to be. His son became a lefty out of spite, playfulness, contempt for swells, and, perhaps most important, desire to meet girls. Leader has explained that the Club, just before Amis's time there, had had a defection by the non-Communist members. The group that Amis joined and supported was solidly Communist and our man joined the Party in 1941. He had a go at Marx and Lenin and other texts, but the studious and dedicated part sounds much less convincing than the sex. True he wanted good housing and jobs (and jazz and fun) for all; but it's also true that he was busy bedding a serious young comrade. After he lost his virginity, she recommended a lovemaking manual by a Dutchman. Amis was out of face and very annoyed. Along with his pals he tried a more congenial form of rebellion than politics—a naysayers' support group, as it were. English undergraduates have always loved their exclusive groups—intellectual like the Cambridge Apostles (very smart and very nice), political/literary like the Auden circle (intense about changing the world), aesthetic and a bit frivolous (like the connoisseurs of the Harold Acton/Brian Howard era). The Seven—whose motto was SUMUS (I AM)—was a swaggering association, devoted to assertive blokishness. Norman Iles, as Leader has shown us, was surely the group's most clear spokesman. His manifesto needs to be quoted in full:

> "We are" is an answer to "You are not." It was an answer to the Dean of the College, to academic learning, to our homes and parents, to the rules of society, and to the war itself. All these cried. "You are not." "We are," we replied. In addition it meant this. We are ourselves, whole, and will grow whole. We are greater than learning, intellect, convention and desire to get on in life. It had the idea of ourselves as natural forces, growing as a flower does—or as a tree.

These men also added a campy kind of banter to their truculence. Amis called Larkin "dalling," and Larkin signed a letter to his pal "Your loving wife, Doris." Yet homosexual activity was not in the mix: it was transgressive play, being louche and bad—adding every kind of verbal and gestural insult for an assault on the social system. Amis had his picture taken with some of the Seven holding an "invisible dagger," about to plunge it into an imaginary enemy. In a letter to Larkin he expatiated on the pleasures of being awful; it all sounds like a Brit version of Dostoyevsky's *Underground Man*, except that there's no veneer of politeness or conventionality. Amis also does not seem to be in pain as a result of his nastiness—he wallows comfortably in his defects. With Larkin he can "admit to shady, dishonest, crawling cowardly, brutal, unjust, arrogant, lecherous, perverted, and generally shameful feelings" that he wouldn't want known by others. The only inconsistency here is that he was acting out a good bit of his nasty side—far from being top secret it spread to his whole life and career. He and Larkin were "savagely uninterested" in the same things—and both were to establish themselves as writers who didn't pay attention to or couldn't stand most of the hum and buzz of high and low culture. Between them they hated or were indifferent to many famous painters, writers, musicians, and public figures of their time.

Meanwhile there was a war on and Amis was soon serving in the Signal Corp from 1942–45. The break in his Oxford career was by no means a shattering experience. Surprisingly enough, given his dislike of authority, Amis did well in the army during his 3 year service. He didn't mind the discipline, the drilling, and he loved the camaraderie. What he didn't like was the "ignorant jumped up so called bloody gentlemen" who were the senior officers. They were snobbish, obsessed with appearances, and only got where they were because of "quick promotion" in wartime. Amis—whatever can be said against him—was always concerned with substance, hard work, quality, and no frills.

When he returned to the University, he soon met a pretty art student from Ruskin College named Hilary Bardwell. He began courting her with a kind of rude directness, not to say obnoxiousness. He wore a hairy ginger-colored tweed jacket and policeman's pants on dates and specialized in making negative comments on the people who came into the tearoom where they met. "Look at those fools, look at that idiot of a man" is a typical Amis line. Meanwhile gentle Hilly, a girl who liked jazz and painting and a good laugh, was "dippy" about him even though he didn't at all like "the heavy stuff of romance." He preferred to date in a group and could tell funny stories and get everyone roaring. He was also wavy haired, quite handsome and dynamic—and filled with knowledge of poetry and writing, even while disdaining the role of the teacher. She knew he was a forceful presence, but had trouble with the nastiness. When she gave him the air for a time, he found her in the Ashmolean trying to make a sketch of "one of those Greek stone chaps." They got back together. With very little self-esteem (only glad to "get a chap interested in me") she gave into him sexually and she was pregnant when they married.

Hilly's father was another object for Amis's aggression. He was a social cut above Daddy A and earned a living as a civil servant for the Ministry of Agriculture. He was also a lover of folk music, an all-round camper and outdoorsman, a man who had learned several exotic languages such as Romany, Swedish, and Welsh. He wore a beret. Amis pronounced him, in his memoirs, "an extraordinary old man like a music loving lavatory attendant." (Grandson Martin confirms this observation.) He would model the buffoonish Professor Welch in *Lucky Jim* after Daddy B. Amis was perfectly willing to admit that he hated "anybody who does anything UNUSUAL at ALL." So what this amounts to is that he hated the chintz and the rabbit ornaments as well as the foreign inflections of bohemia. He would necessarily have to position himself carefully in order to avoid a good many people. He would have to discover the right locale to be comfortable.

Oxford, as indicated, was the right and wrong place for him: there were pals to make common cause with and there were dons

to be endured. Among the former—not counting the Seven—
were the future drama critic Kenneth Tynan and the future novelist John Wain. Tynan, son of a nouveau riche business man and
a working-class woman, was at a grander college, Magdalen. He
was cutting a figure as a latter-day dandy and aesthete. His velvet
suits, damasked shirts and love of the elegant Randolph Hotel
bar were things that set him apart from the rough-hewn Amis,
but the latter spotted him as an anti-Establishment type. He was
making a name at the Oxford Playhouse as an actor and making
a big impression as a campy, "womanish" player of a role—the
part of Kenneth Tynan, wit and transgressor. Tynan had a dissolute reputation which fascinated Amis—but the nature of this
was by no means entirely homosexual. Amis delighted in the fact
that Tynan was a "say dissed" and enjoyed playing teacher and
"SKOOLGERL" with a young lady who was a "mass o' kissed."
His life and work is a monument to blokedom which we will get
to later on. John Wain, a well-heeled undergraduate at St John's,
established a magazine called *The Mandrake* which had as its mission to "oppose sham and cant . . . by quietly fostering honest
workmanship." While Amis never published there, he did develop
a friendship of sorts with Wain, consisting of mutual support and
jocular competitiveness. Wain's novel *Hurry on Down* came out
a year before *Lucky Jim* and featured a well-educated but out-of-
step protagonist intent upon defying middle-class standards. Jim,
as we shall see, is not an entirely dissimilar young academic who
can't abide his awful bourgeois colleagues. Wain was to help Amis
when he was at the BBC and devoted a program to his old school-
mate's new novel; but he was also to give Amis digs of the are-
you-writing-anything-these-days sort. Another chum was Bruce
Montgomery, known as the mystery writer "Edmund Crispin."
This ultra-sophisticate appealed to Amis because his caustic wit
could cut through received literary opinion and get to the heart
of what was worth reading. And then there was James Michie,
a Trinity man and poet who talked about verse technique with

Amis—both men valued clarity. Together they put out an anthology of university poets titled *Oxford Poetry*. Zachary Leader remarks that the verse that they brought together is notable for its specificity and hardness, qualities that characterize Amis's writing in the years to come.

The most awful don that Amis ever dealt with was the very famous Lord David Cecil, younger son of the Marquess of Salisbury. After getting a First in the Schools in 1947—proving that he could master a mountain of (to him) unpalatable English literature—Amis decided to go for the B.Litt in hopes of making a living as an academic. His memoirs contain a hilarious account of trying to work with Lord David as his sponsor. The great man, author of impressionistic books of criticism, was too great to be located for advisement at his college. His specialty was the pretentious lecture. Amis's gift for mimicry is at its height as he records Cecil's patrician throat-clearing and time-wasting: "Laze . . . laze ands gentlemen, when we say a man looks like a poet . . . dough mean . . . looks like Chauthah . . . dough mean . . . looks like Dvyden." Down the road Cecil was to play a part in the rejection of Amis's thesis on the Pre-Raphaelites and the nature of nineteenth-century audience reception. This would be a hot topic today, but back then it was considered unsound and unscholarly.

Sent away without that degree, Amis nevertheless plunged into the unglamorous regions of academe. He spent a dozen years at the University of Swansea—awash in student papers, lectures to be prepared, extramarital affairs, heroic drinking, and very serious writing of funny novels. Philip Larkin encouraged him and gave advice about a piece of fiction called "Dixon and Christine." That manuscript eventually became his ticket to fame, if not immediate fortune.

Lucky Jim, published in 1954, was the most famous post-World War II novel about The Condition of England, not the old nineteenth century issue of the haves and have-nots but the new issue of the vital struggling with the dreary. People were not perishing in the backstreets of Manchester, but they were living desperately dull lives. Jim Dixon, the new man at a provincial university, was sent by Kingsley Amis to disturb an array of half-alive academic fuddy duddies, arty poseurs, frustrated single women, rigid matrons. *Lucky Jim* came out 3 years after Salinger's *Catcher in the Rye* and has the same strange, enduring appeal. It's about someone half-cracked who sees the awfulness of comfortable middle-class routine. Jim is England's Holden, with a university degree but no intention of obliging superiors, accepting received opinion, or doing anything besides messing up. And both books share a critical problem. How do we wind up accepting the perceptions, tastes, and standards of an incompetent? Jim, from the start, is an educator against education, someone who's a medievalist and hates scholarly study of the Middle Ages. What makes his antics, his gorilla imitation, his lying, his destruction of property, his nastiness, and sexism so appealing? For someone whose motto is "nice things are nicer than nasty ones" he seems, to say the least, a bit of a problem.

The problem has two parts: the nature of the awfulness (nastiness, as Jim calls it) that surrounds our protagonist and our protagonist's awfulness. The first is pinned down by Amis in the specific descriptions of academic life and the personnel involved. Begin with a concert that Jim attends when he gets his new job: "A soporific droning filled the air round Dixon as the singers hummed their notes to one another." Professor Welch, who is Jim's exacting, pedantic boss, has introduced the music this way: "Of course, this sort of music is not intended for an audience, you see." Welch starts the madrigal with his "arthritic forefinger" and the performers, including a fussy woman named Margaret who fancies Jim, "sing away." The lyrics run to lines like "When from my love I looked for love, and kind affections due." Jim can't help wondering what would make this line apply to him and Margaret. The false, absurd, pretentious, windy occasion—music making with no intention of reaching an audience—is a fine example of Amis's

awful vision. Such things are Amis's specialty: at the very beginning of the book Welch going on about some ridiculous distinction between a flute and a recorder, filling the air with nit-picking.
Jim imagines what the two of them should appear like to passing
students: professors discussing history. In fact they are so far from
anything with substance—so mired in trivia—that Jim begins
to daydream about a real discussion. The strategy in both Amis
scenes is quite similar to Salinger's when he has Holden reporting to a teacher about a badly written exam: the young boy gets
a cant-ridden lecture about playing the game and not playing the
game. He knows he's out of sync with what's expected, but what's
expected is useless nonsense. Jim Dixon is trapped in a world of
awful things and people and must fight his way out, using every
form of aggression at his disposal. Holden Caulfield goes AWOL;
Jim mutters, makes his famous Evelyn Waugh face, does his
Martian imitations, ventilates, transgresses, gets blind drunk, and
does something awful at an awful public lecture. As we shall see,
he loses his position at the college by breaking down entirely and
lapsing into nonsense that goes academic nonsense one better. His
whole story in the book is about finding creative ways of getting
back, being worse than the intolerable people around him.

The people who surround Jim—like those who tic off Holden
Caulfield—have just the right looks, traits, phrases to tic off a
chap who likes a beer, a pretty woman, and a good read. They live
in a land of pretense, a place where false phrases and appearances
dominate. Take Margaret, a faculty member who has recently been
jilted by a fellow named Catchpole; she botched an attempt to do
away with herself and is presently pressing Jim hard for attention.
She's "small, thin, and bespectacled," sings in the Conservative
Association choir (recall Daddy A), and inclined to ask him questions such as "Am I the only girl you know in this place?" Jim says
that he values "honesty and straightforwardness" as the only relief
in "the awful business of getting along with women." Margaret
provides manipulation and artifice, including a terrifically funny

fit of hysterics later in the book. Amis goes into Jim's head and tells us exactly what's wrong with the woman. Jim is rueful about his grim romantic fate: "The huge class that contained Margaret was destined to provide his own womenfolk: those with whom the intention of being attractive could sometimes be made to get itself confused with performance; those with whom a too-tight skirt, a wrong-coloured, or no, lipstick, even an ill-executed smile could instantly discredit that illusion beyond apparent renewal of hope." The thoughts are cruel—part of Jim's campaign of getting back—but they have an authentic ring. So does his remark that he could praise any of her outfits except the "green Paisley frock in combination with the low-heeled, quasi-velvet shoes." This is bloke short-hand for give-me-honest-attractiveness, something the main love interest Christine has in full measure.

The complication is that Christine is attached to the book's greatest poseur, Welch's artist son Bertrand. He wears a yellow sport jacket, has a large beard, and one of his first lines in the book is "it's very pleasant to come down here and to know that the torch of culture is still in a state of combustion in the provinces." He and Jim butt heads throughout the book, the phony aesthete and the struggling chap with a living to get. The blowout scene involves Jim exposing Bertrand for what he is—"a twister and a snob and a bully and a fool." Bertrand has two-timed the beautiful Christine, engaged in the "old slap and tickle" with a married woman. He's no sensitive artist, only a "touchy and vain" character who's taken up with himself. And Jim—short-legged and not prepossessing—actually exchanges blows with him, indeed knocks him down. He pronounces his tall, well-built opponent "a totem pole on a crap reservation." Other characters are also anti-Dixon. Welch's wife is censorious, a battleaxe—and Jim has been the unideal houseguest who burned a hole in a quilt when drunk. The brightest student around is an earnest young man who wants Jim to offer a special medieval course; the only trouble is that the readings this fellow wants to consider would cause two pretty

girls to drop out. Pretense, manipulation, bullying, scolding—
and scaring off girls. These are serious vices in the Amis world.

Added to this is Jim's problem with the nature of his work:
like Amis himself, he's a critical reader and a man of learning, but
he's not cut out to be a conventional scholar with a field. A field,
like a pretentious presentation, is the worst thing you can have.
It hems you in, sums you up, allows you to earn a living, but not
to live. Jim posits that we all go in for what we hate most. In his
case he's written an article on medieval ship building, agreed to
give courses in areas of the Middle Ages that make his eyes glaze
over, allowed himself to be bullied into giving a public lecture on
Merrie England. And what's so bad about all that? Leader quotes
a real don who thought the ship building was perfectly good. The
answer here is that the wrong people do these things—pedants
and makers of fine distinctions, those who are in touch with fuss-
iness not fun, with artificial distinctions rather than gut reactions.
Philistine, of course, but also charged with passion. Here's Jim
on the Middle Ages: "The hydrogen bomb, the South African
Government, Chiang Kai-shek, Senator McCarthy himself would
then seem a light price to pay for no longer being in the Middle
Ages. Had people ever been as nasty, as self-indulgent, as dull, as
miserable, as cocksure, as bad at art, as ludicrous."

The railing and bombast are an attempt to break through to
an Amis truth: what's well established in high places is well worth
attacking. In his disastrous public lecture Jim—blotto on sherry
and whisky—shows what he thinks of Merrie England. At first
he assumes the tone of Professor Welch, throwing in every windy
qualification ("as you might call it") and cant phrase ("identifica-
tion of work with craft," "integration of the social consciousness")
that he can think of. Soon he plunges headlong into a snarling
denunciation of "the most un-Merrie period in our history. It's
only the homemade pottery crowd, the organic husbandry crowd,
the recorder-playing crowd, the Esperanto." The tirade isn't far
from American critic Harold Rosenberg's famous attack on the

"herd of independent minds," those trendies who wanted to lay down the law in the cultural realm.

Jim's other big grievances are against depth psychology and literary modernism. The first wants to explore the causes of attraction and love, "indulging in an orgy of emotional self-catechizing about how you know you're in love." From Jim's point of view that's a no-brainer—it's pure instinct and sensation, that nice feeling he gets when he's near Christine. Cut the analysis and fine distinctions. While he's at it Amis also cuts modernist introspection—Rilke, Gide, and Lytton Strachey are almost curse words, meant to suggest dithering indecisiveness and confusion about one's own feelings. Welch and Bertrand are likened to the latter two on the final page of the book. Bloomsbury—where G. E. Moore and E. M. Forster once philosophized about personal relations and the supreme value of art—is also dismissed in a line. Jim knows what he wants, crude and rude as he may be. He's nasty in pursuit of the nice, the pleasurable, the natural.

John Lewis, the librarian protagonist of Amis's second novel *That Uncertain Feeling*, is a family man and not as out of control as Jim. His drinking is not a problem but his mouth, his sensibilities, and his roving eye are. Why does he prolong a conversation with young Dilys: "Dilys was a girl, a fact not lightly to be put aside. In the second place, it was because she was on the right side of the line dividing the attractive from the rest." Take that. In the town where he works he and his wife socialize with the successful local professionals and have "bits of things to eat on sticks" at parties. The uncomfortable phrasing here—blokespeak about most gatherings—is one of the best features of the book. It's all about that uncertain feeling you get when you're where you don't belong, doing what you shouldn't be doing. Mrs. Lewis begs him to cut the Karl Marx when in company; without her common sense, he'd bawl a defense of the Welfare State and call for a toast for Comrade Malenkov. There's nothing behind this but Schadenfreude and a love of matey rather than tony people. He's not a bit interested in the price of used sports cars. "How could these people so much as move about, weighed down as they were in their Field Service Marching Order of boredom?" This is not the tedium of college teachers, but of high-paid dentists.

A fetching woman named Elizabeth Gruffydd-William, wife of a rich businessman, provides the break from dreariness. She's arty, interested in the history of Welsh costuming, and ultimately offensive to Lewis's basic decency. He'd like to fool with Elizabeth, and he goes a bit down that road by running around town for meetings and drinks. But his heart isn't in adultery and being a rakehell: he feels "rather a good chap for not liking myself for it, and not liking myself at all for feeling a good chap." That's the uncertain feeling—disliking the underhanded and disliking yourself for being complacent. Elizabeth, besides wanting sex, wants to use crooked means to get Jim the big job at the library. That's a "fiddle," Jim says and he doesn't do fiddles; they bother you, go against your instincts. It's not that he's morally scrupulous, but he can't commit to dishonesty. He's out for a bit of fun, not a scheme. He's not "a twister" like Lucky Jim's nemesis Bertrand. Characteristically, when he's being bad, we see him escaping in disguise from Elizabeth's house dressed in a woman's period costume. An old man on a bus hits on him.

John Lewis also can't commit to all the pretense and flummery that goes with his librarian's job. Amis—in a wonderfully detailed way—shows how a job in the culture and literacy industry takes it out of an honest man. He's forced into the company of Gareth Probert, the town's famous poet and a fabulous send-up of Dylan Thomas. John feels he's a "scruff" who is "court poet" to the gentry, a windy bore who sounds like "Owain Glyndwr in a play on the welsh Children's Hour." John has to sit through a performance of Probert's play *The Martyr*, an excruciating historical piece that has lines like "Angels on horseback wept with vinegar." John has little taste for bards generally, "wild valley babblers, wadded with pit dirt and sheep shit." Nor is he good at the politics of culture. At the library one needs, in order to advance, to placate the high-horse gentry and the down-to-earth trade unionists who serve as overseers. One would think, given John's leftward leanings, that the latter would be to his taste. But he finds one old man's literal minded talk about "the public"—and what that working-class abstraction wants—to be extremely annoying. Lewis, no snob, nevertheless, refers to the fellow's "blunt bus conductor's face" and his humorlessness. Things only seem good at the pub, where "the new privileged classes," grocers and butchers in blue blazers, are better than the old privileged. Highfalutin is bad, down to earth is bad. Good is located somewhere in the comfortable middle.

John abandons the library at the end for a job in coal sales. He and his wife are once again asked out to a gathering where their hostess, the butcher's wife, gives them "a lovely warm hug." But don't think Lewis is completely satisfied. Even here he has to listen to a discourse from a professor about the "switches" that control social motivation. Even here he gets "sherry that tasted like the brine those pickled herrings are bottled in, plus a scintilla of dishcloth." The only answer appears to be the last scene in which he and his wife go into the pub with the miners going off shift. This is to say that Amis can't quite make up his mind about what's the best part of bloke life. Maybe it's just the pleasures of the moment.

In any event, it's not exotic adventure or new sensations. *I Like It Here* (1958) is a sarcastic look at what many Brits were yearning for in the gray 1950s—fun in a southern clime, new tastes, and sights. The book is about finding an honest space between dreary conventionality and all the hype about "abroadness." Garnet Bowen, a writer who has a (money-making) idea for a travel piece, is annoyed when an editor is actually interested in the idea. His publisher also gets him involved in a mission to track down a famous writer who may or may not be living in Portugal: is the "author" of a manuscript received by the firm really by the great man or a hoaxer? Off Bowen goes to "abroad," grumbling from the start about the famous writer: "Why can't he live in England like everyone else?"

The social origin of his resentment is the "long history of lower-middle-class envy directed against the upper middle class traveler" who did things in style, knew the right hotel and stayed with a contessa. But deeper than that is a blokish feeling about overrated things, the Amis attitude toward classics and monuments. Abroad was no more "beautiful or significant than a Pimlico bus station"; it gave you insight into yourself, perhaps, but so would "a sharp go of locomotor ataxia." "All that sun" made you "get out" instead of "keeping quiet and getting on with the job." The architecture was a bore and more than that there was nothing to do there. Once again, the fuming and jabbing are at one and the same time very funny and irritating. "Lisbon was all right, and would be really worth while if it could somehow be got on rollers and shifted to about half-way between Brighton and Eastbourne." If a great city like Lisbon is overrated—and the distinctness of a culture is overrated—what's justly rated? Amis's protagonist backs off from any "disrespect to the Portuguese" (who are just chaps going about their business), but he stands firm on "filthy goat's milk cheese" and other put-downs about "their" daily life. He wants us to think that he is an occupant of the reasonable and decent and measured middle ground— nothing weird or unusual or attention-grabbing.

All the while, however, he's making himself rather conspicuous and not a little bit obnoxious. His wife Barbara thinks his love of English beer is a kind of aggressive posturing: "it was working class, British, lower-middle class, Welsh, anti-foreign, anti-upper-class, anti-London, anti-intellectual, British and proletarian." It is a form of verbal brawling, if truth be told: he enjoys the fantasy of inventing "Bowen's Beer" and designing an advertisement with a picture of his mother-in-law drinking a lot of it. The lettering at the bottom would be "Makes You Drunk." Bowen uses a similar hammering style to drive home his point about moral seriousness in writing. Henry Fielding, whose grave Bowen visits in Lisbon, is the "only non-contemporary novelist who could be read with unaffected and whole-hearted interest" 200 years later. Duty is plain in his work, as is malevolence. Such "a simplified world" comforts Bowen; it has ethical weight without "the aid of evangelical puffing and blowing." This mini-lecture has the virtue of directness and honesty, but it's hardly more than attitudinizing. Amis is having a bracing good time telling us what to think, using his own brand of puffing. What makes this more tolerable than a sermon is the brisk pace, sharp phasing, and desire to distance himself from mealy-mouthed conventionality.

Each visitor to Amis's bloke world will have to decide whether he finds the conclusions of *I Like It Here* insightful or bullying. Bowen returns to England, having solved the mystery of who wrote the manuscript. (He uses the test of pomposity on the author; someone this awful, this self-important, can't be putting on an act when he says he wrote the book.) Bowen hopes to get a job with the publishing house because he needs the money; but "a frightful little turd of a failed barrister" gets the position. In any case, Bowen is glad to accept his own "closed mind" and to realize how much he likes it here. He sees the "rear elevation" of a female book critic getting into a taxi and wants to kick it.

A better novel, but a nastier one, is *Take a Girl Like You*, which came out in 1960 and in its own way crystallizes a do-what-you feel hedonistic attitude that's quite different from counterculture hedonism. There's nothing more than male neediness and animal nature in the philosophy of the protagonist; he never gets cosmic, keeps away from the silliness of *Playboy* philosophy, sticks to everyday lust. The lack of grandiosity, glamour, and earnest pleading for sexual liberation makes the book a straightforward cry for a good time. It's also honest about the awfulness of young Patrick Standish, a teacher of classics who is shown getting what he wants in a fairly gross way. While no one is sad or ruined or about to engage in agonizing moral huffing and puffing, the characters are laid bare by Amis, with no hint of making them brave pioneers in the sexual revolution. And while Standish is pretty nasty, he is not without a conscience, an ability to see his nature and its limits. Blokes are not lowlifes; they simply lack all the delicate equipment of romantics.

Patrick meets young Jenny Bunn, also a teacher in a little English town in one of the southern counties. She's from up North and has a mix of attitudes that drives Patrick crazy: she's old fashioned about pre-marital sex but keen on clothes, dancing, and going out with blokes. The inhibitions, Patrick thinks, would make sense if she liked sewing meetings or had a mustache, but she's smashing. Patrick has a reputation for being "quite a lad for the old hoo-ha"; Jenny comes direct from a family circle, a dad who's a bit strict and a grandma whose house is filled with sounds of hymns "of the sort that made you want to do away with yourself," viz. "King of Love My Shepherd Is" and "There Is a Green Hill far Away." Patrick and Jenny date; he puts immediate moves on her and is rebuffed. The rest of the book is like a loopy version of Samuel Richardson's *Clarissa*—a very nice girl winds up getting, by any reasonable definition, raped. Jenny is drunk and helpless at the time, and Patrick won't be put off any longer. And she winds up accepting the naturalness of male brutality. The book is a see-what-we-mean gift to feminists, of course; but it's also something else—a study of the twists and turns of British maleness, many states of mind that are more than lustful.

In Standish's case we begin with familiar things: life is all right really and death is something as boring as "the history of banking." The Common Room in the Master's Lodge of a boys' school is a hideous place "notable for the absence of naked women and tanks of gin." And love "testified to a certain emotional refinement, which, like thrift, courage, and veracity, he had often suspected to be foreign to his nature." Jenny even admires his lack of refinement: it's "energetic, eager, confiding, shrewd, enjoying himself, intimate in the cool scoffing way she loved." But that's not the last word on feelings. There's something that eats away at Patrick's swagger, keeps him from fully enjoying himself in the way an unreflective cad would; for all his randiness, he can't help but admit he's missed out on a lot because of a "lack of unscrupulousness." He doesn't like to think about this dereliction of male duty, but it's a fact. Amis underscores this on several occasions. A kind of morality is never far away; it ruins the pursuit of satiety; it makes Patrick nervous. He doesn't quite like the real, raw sexual kind of woman either. Taste and temperament—what he likes (Jenny) and what he is prone to (anyone willing)—are at war. And he was spending far more time trying not to be bad than trying not to be nasty—this higher aspiration was, he comments, getting to be annoying. But it was part of his nature. *Take a Girl Like You* is about how very stressful it is to be nasty; ultimately someone like Patrick is going to do something awful and start to hate himself. Any reader of the book is likely to note that while Patrick is not agonizing about his behavior, he's hardly at ease. It's decent conscience and scruples kicking in. Now, granted, this is not a very big moral breakthrough and seems like an easy game for a seducer. But Amis never glosses over Patrick's brutality and dishonesty; on the other hand, he never lets us forget his male impatience with the woman's game of holding out when she'd like to go for it.

Meanwhile, Jenny herself has some blokish qualities, one of them being the good warm sensation she gets when Patrick is near: it opened up the world, "gave you all sorts of new feelings you would have no idea existed otherwise." Or put another way, "She had a sort of permanent two gin and tonics inside her." And the ending has her in quite good humor as she gets her man and admits that the old Bible school precepts have taken a knocking. "[T]hey were bound to . . . with a girl like you," Patrick answers.

Roger Micheldene, the main character in *One Fat Englishman*, is Amis's totally awful bloke on the loose. The other characters—especially Jim Dixon and John Bowen—can be quite nice fellows, but Roger isn't even trying to be nice. Which is not to say that he has no self-knowledge: he recognizes his own self-ishness, accepts himself, and yet sees no "need of working the whole thing up into a philosophy." The title's meaning gives away a lot: a woman whom Roger is making love to—that is, nearly crushing—refers to him as one fat Englishman.

On publisher's business in America, Roger is yet another Amis character whose faults are thrown into high relief because he's not where he should be. Again, abroad. Most of the action takes place at Budweiser University (modeled on Princeton), a school with a predictable amount of bed-hopping and backbiting. Roger is supposed to be giving talks and looking for talent, but actually he's most involved with trying to resume an affair with a woman presently married to a Danish professor. Helene Bang is a lovely creature with a petite figure and perfect teeth—and a strange willingness to submit to one of the most obnoxious fellows in the modern English literary canon. Micheldene is a lustful, rude gourmand with a peremptory manner, a tendency to wallow hap-pily in his faults, and a bad British take on everything American. ("[He] could have done with less of their habit of hanging up an Audubon print wherever they felt like it . . . any fool who owned half a continent was going to own a lot of birds and mammals and such as well. They ought to have got over all that by now.")

The book is contrived in the extreme—with Roger humbled by a witty Jewish writer at the school and punished even more severely by having to return to Britain on shipboard with an awful American Anglophile who talks nonsense for the duration. The real point of the novel is to showcase the variety of Roger's nasty talents. Name it and he's got it. We hear of the "Yid scrib-bler" and his love of sadism in fiction, novelistic scenes that mock blind people. But this comes from someone who has perfected the art of the nasty put-down. He may not agree with the trendy Jewish writer's philosophy of doing what you like—irrespective of the consequences—but that demurral is totally empty. He's not liberated in that 1960s way, but his gross inconsiderateness is doing-what-you-like under a different guise. The book could have been called *The Joys of Awfulness*—Roger eating and screwing and insulting his way through the pages, with the delights of every encounter recorded in detail. He takes snuff, is condescending about the best cigar in the Queen's Tavern, is proud of his "wide and deep lap" which could "accommodate indefinitely a girl far bulkier than Helene." And then there's the sheer fun of domination: "there was something masterful as well about the idea of a lap." When he's at his worst he feels "great waves of power flooding in toward him."

"Why are you so awful?" Helene asks him at one point. And Roger gets serious and sober for a bit. It's because he's a snob, rebelling against his vulgar father, a hopeless lover of fast cars and the radio. The latter, it seems, had in his turn rebelled against a rich father who collected pictures and had real taste; Roger would like to get back to that part of his heritage and does everything he can to sneer at modernity in all its forms. There's more than a touch of Evelyn Waugh in this contempt. Take Roger's opinion of the American turnpike: "By having so many tons of metal hurtling along at these speeds, you see, hooting, winking, overtaking, they hoped to convince themselves and one another that they had energy and were important and were going somewhere." The old master himself—with his ear trumpet, his love of cigars, and his irascibility—couldn't have said it better. And the old master was very aware of his own awfulness—just as Roger is. Add to this that Roger's a Roman Catholic and enjoys baiting an American clergyman named Father Colgate at Budweiser who is a popular preacher and go-getter. Roger, in true Waugh fashion, berates him for his meretricious with-it quality. "Your sensibility's been packaged and air-conditioned and refrigerated out of existence." Colgate is accused of flattering "commuter communicants," serving a "neon Christ," and giving a Hail Mary as penance for every

Martini after the third. Now Amis himself doesn't quite endorse Roger's guff; he makes the Jewish novelist say it sounds like bad Graham Greene. But the fact is that Roger gets off a few good lines as he lectures the showy Colgate: "Is your imagination so puny that the vast terror and horror of the mystery [of the universe] simply passes you by altogether?" Roger sees American faith as "half-baked humanitarianism" and the American God as a "corporation president" worried about "group morale and togetherness." Amis—an atheist to the core of his being—nevertheless enjoys making his protagonist someone who believes in terror rather than togetherness. The harshness of true belief can sort well with the harshness of the bloke.

Many years later Amis was a member of the Garrick Club but in certain ways he was still One Fat Englishman—a blend of the jolly and the curmudgeonly, the rather nasty and intolerant, the rude. If truth be told he wasn't an ideal clubman—couldn't tolerate and talk to bores, couldn't keep away from the anti-woman remarks, couldn't be depended on to blend his cheerfulness with civility. The novelist Keith Waterhouse tried to make excuses for him and he of course—due to his fame—had plenty of respectful listeners in the coffee room and at the bar. He also loved the place, as he wrote to Larkin: "Somewhere to get pissed in jovial very literary all-male company." (This of course sounds more like a writers' and artists' pub than a club.)

Now Judy Hough, a friend whom Amis's biographer Zachary Leader quotes, is not necessarily the most reliable witness of the novelist's behavior and, well, his literary ethos. She knew him in his old age when he was the redoubtable clubman and the most famous writer in Britain; she was married to his close writer friend Richard Hough and spent many an evening with him. There's something that rings true in her plain remark: "He got into the habit of behaving badly." And unless you want to make ridiculous claims for authorial distance, he is a writer who got into the habit of ventilating and sounding off in his books. Please don't forget the basic crude aggression in Jim and his other early protagonists, people who are—as the theorists say—privileged within the stories. But it's also true that Amis's badness brings all sorts of truths to light: his colorful disregard for convention and politeness allows us to see bores and hypocrites and trendies and poseurs and time servers and young seducers for what they are.

4

John Osborne

John Osborne, the theatrical bloke par excellence, was not only famous for his plays but for the play that was his life: of the pioneering writers in this book, Osborne is by far the most flamboyant, outrageous, startling, and dangerous to know. His dramas, autobiographical volumes, declarations, notebooks—and his daily life from dreary boyhood to in-your-face artistic success to celebrity marriages—were one long assault on English convention, restraint, and decency. He didn't write about a situation or live a moment without managing to rub someone the wrong way, hit a live nerve in an audience. His specialty was grand-scale giving and taking offense.

George Orwell's famous essay "Why I Write"—a proto-bloke revolution document—is a good way to get into the Osborne world. In describing what's behind his literary life Orwell writes about verbal facility and "a power of facing unpleasant facts"; both are Osborne trademarks. Osborne was always an avid devourer of encyclopedias and dictionaries, a word lover whose shabby education was compensated for by extensive, if random, reading and apprentice writing. The facts of his London and suburban daily life became the spirit and the material of his plays—the tubercular father who died at the age of 39; the whining, life-denying mother who never missed a chance to discourage her son; the set of awful relatives, mostly hard-bitten or indifferent; the off-color patter of the music hall performer Max Miller.

Orwell's motives for writing are a close fit with Osborne's inner drives. There's "Sheer egoism," which includes "Desire to seem clever, to be talked about, to be remembered after death, to get your own back on grownups who snubbed you in childhood, etc., etc." Osborne was big on recrimination, revenge, denunciation, self-assertion at the expense of those who were stupid or insensitive or ludicrous. One of his relatives threatened to sue him for his portrait of his maternal grandmother. His first successful play, *Look Back in Anger*, gets back at his first wife. Telling people off—from a stage, a page, from school, or the South of France—was his art form. "Damn You, England," perhaps the most uncivil literary response to a public question written by a twentieth-century figure, was a piece about the idiotic defense of nuclear weaponry, sent to a newspaper. He also delighted in quoting himself, in writing broadsides, in conducting his sexual career for the benefit of the newspapers. "Esthetic enthusiasm" is another Orwell motive—the pleasure that comes from "the right arrangement" of words. Osborne's plays and his prose are filled with gripping rhetoric, speeches that pull an audience into his tumultuous, emotionally conflicted world. Jimmy Porter in *Look Back in Anger*, the marathon talker without a decent job; Archie Rice in *The Entertainer*, the washed up music hall performer; *Luther*, the man of the Book and the indictment; and Bill Maitland in *Inadmissible Evidence*, the solicitor who lays out the facts of his own anguish: each belongs among the most convincing monologists in modern English drama. They arrange things so that we believe in their agonies. Orwell's penultimate motive—"Desire to see things as they are"—is perfect for Osborne's writing and life: he took English drama out of the drawing room into the bedsitter; his props were ironing boards and cheesy music hall sets, not sherry decanters. The last Orwellian motive—"Political purpose"—is "the desire to push the world in a certain direction"; in Orwell's case that meant "a hatred of authority," a sympathy for the working classes, and a keen sense of injustice. The first and third apply to Osborne—but if truth be told, they apply without Orwell's high principles, without the integrity. Osborne was a rebel and a malcontent—championing vague things like honesty, affection, the primacy of one's own perceptions—not a democratic socialist with unselfish ideas about the public good. Yet Orwell is a good starting point for an understanding of this bloke because they share the desire to force their unpleasant truths on an audience and "push the world in a certain direction."

A Better Class of Person, the first volume of Osborne's autobiography, is one of the classic texts of bloke life—almost everything you want to know (but are uncomfortable when you know it) about growing up resentful, poor, and lower middle class in Britain during the 1930s and 1940s. It's a young male's story of trying to be a self against the backdrop of family squabbling, hurt feelings, bad schools, lost friendships, childhood illness, and English life without the English coziness, security, and tradition that we've all heard so much about. Osborne performs the feat of making drabness fascinating. He adds to the fund of toughs, dreamers, and schemers in V. S. Pritchett's *A Cab at the Door*, that classic about lower middle-class Edwardian life; but he does even more with those who have been wounded by class and the darker side of the national temperament. His mother is the villain of the piece: not exactly like Dickens's mother—anxious for her son to go back to a drudge's life working in a blacking factory—but close to it. Nellie Beatrice (born Grove) was the child of a once prosperous pub owner and a woman in charge of the cleaning staff at Woolworth's. She went to work as an adolescent and at 16 became (remarkably) head cashier at a branch of the ur-chain restaurant Lyons Corner in the Strand. Perhaps following family tradition she thereafter earned a living as a barmaid—and had quite a reputation for conviviality, good humor, and the ability to draw a pint with style and juggle beer bottles. She had a buoyant, off-color line of patter—especially in her heyday during the war, when tips from American soldiers were big and the going was good ("One Yank and they're off!" is typical). This front load of bonhomie had darkness behind it—what Osborne called "Black Looks." Her son and sick husband were treated to a dour, defeat-ist, sneering attitude toward the world. Every nationality has its version of whining, bitching, and dampening of the spirit; the lower middle-class British version is particularly offensive to the developing male ego: it's all about nothing being anything much, no one caring for you and why should you care for them, no place to go in life and only pathetic hopes waiting to be dashed. These are the sounds of defeat that echoed in Osborne's young life—the ones that made him the aggressor he became.

"Comfort in the discomfort of others was an abiding family recreation," Osborne wrote of his mother's family, the Groves. They lived in Fulham Palace Road, "amid a succession of identi-cal streets, Victorian terraced houses with strange little gnarled cigar stubs of trees lining the pavements." Grandma Grove—"a tough, sly old Cockney, with a harsh, often cruel wit"—set the tone: she had "come down in the world" (a big family theme) in that her husband had once been the owner of a flashy pubic house; he lost his footing, and Grandma went out as a cleaning woman. She also gained a lifelong topic of conversation—"getting above yourself"—and a nasty way of sneering at others' misfortune. Her sisters and daughter came naturally to this point of view. "If one of them died, fell ill, or short of money it was something to be talked about rather than experienced in common." Osborne called these small-time sadists "The Grove Repertory Company"; he referred to the Grove Family Rows as emerging from "a port-wine haze of unsated disappointment." And he in turn took pleasure in their discomfiture. Anything that could crack open their world pleased him. He delighted in a story about Grandpa Grove in his heyday at the Duncannon, that prosperous pub near

St Martin-in-the-Fields. Marie Lloyd, the great music hall performer, once reeled around the place after a big night; Grandma,
a pregnant young woman, ordered her out. The response: "Don't
you fucking well talk to me! I've just left your old man after a
weekend in Brighton."

Osborne's mother also gets her comeuppance, time after time.
She's exposed for her toxicity: most of it involves poisoning the
affections and dreams of the yearning, curious boy. First and fore-
most, she was a terrible companion to Thomas Godfrey Osborne,
John's father, an ailing man with a great heart and a fine brain.
The mismatched couple had met—where else?—at a pub in the
Strand where she was tending bar. He was an advertising copy-
writer keen on drink; she was a practiced flirt. They married and
made each other miserable—his poor health gave Nellie Beatrice
a further reason to whine, brood, and lash out. The couple was
often separated, with "dad" in hospital. At one point, near the
end of the ordeal, they went to Ventnor on the Isle of Wight,
where the very young boy watched over his father, buying him
Penguin paperbacks for his last Christmas present. John always
felt that his mother didn't care.

Understandably he wanted friends and an escape from the
family. There seemed to be chances when they moved from
Fulham out to Ewell Parade near Epsom. This was a part of
suburbia near Henry VIII's old hunting lodge Nonesuch. John
enjoyed playing Robin Hood games with a local crowd of boys,
relishing the "contemptuous, feared and solitary" part of Sir Guy.
When he found a pal named Joan Buffen—a rather glamorous
little girl who liked horses and dogs and was distinctly genteel—
his mother jeeringly remarked that she couldn't possibly be interested in him. Nellie Beatrice was a strange mix of possessiveness
and brutality; she wanted her son for herself—keeping him out
of school to assuage her own loneliness and boredom—and yet
she wanted him to make fun of, complain about. She mocked
him for his lack of good looks, his childhood ill health, his

attempts to strive for something. She seems like Dickens's Mrs. Joe Gargery—that martyr to childrearing—after a gin and tonic. Osborne mocked her, made literary capital out of her—for a lifetime. He particularly savored a story of Nellie during the Blitz, blown off the lav seat. He described her clothes, those carefully put together lower middle-class rig-outs with everything matching. The flaking makeup and the "dab of California Poppy"— known to kids as eau de dustbins—complete the picture. *A Better Class of Person* retails her anti-Semitism and racism, her bouts of fanatical housecleaning, her restless inability to put down roots and make friends—but strangely we see him staying fairly close to a person he appears to loathe. There's a certain charge to his description of having a cream tea "Up West" with his mother, taking in a picture or one of her favorite music hall performers, Ivor Novello. She's on the scene during his early period of fame after *Look Back in Anger* (even after saying that the write ups weren't very good). She gets to dine with Paul Robeson, an occasion on which she has the chance to tell the great actor that John has always felt very sorry for "darkies." His third wife Penelope Gilliatt and fourth wife Jill Bennett called her "Mum." Osborne let her be depicted on British TV by Eileen Atkins.

But the Grove awfulness was matched by what John experienced with his father's people. The Osbornes were not noisy Cockneys, trading recriminations and insults. They were suburban types of Welsh ancestry who also had come down in the world. Their stock in trade was sheer lifelessness with a dollop of the Groves' spite. They lived in Stoneleigh, a suburb where John and his parents joined them for a time. The place had bland shopping parades, a "station surrounded by a group of housing estates," "Bankclerk's Tudor" architecture. At Grandma Osborne's house John learned about "Routine": "a nice quiet hot drink as usual after yet another nice quiet evening." If Grandma had been any more inactive she would have been ready for the mortuary: she spent her days in an armchair reading Warwick Deeping, taking

a ritual nap, having tea, and smiling her "watery smile." Her husband had been a business failure and lived the life of a whipped
dog. One daughter named Nancy had married pretty well and
her child Tony was held up as a model to the downtrodden boy
John. John's father had been a disappointment—and what was
worse, had once caused the family an expense when he was trying to pursue his artistic ambitions as a young boy. But Grandma
kept such unpleasantness at bay through "a Proper Normal Life,"
the main feature of which was early hours. "Had she been there
she would certainly have made sure that the Last Supper was an
early one."

John's major project—if he were not to sink into the stupor
and spite of family tradition—was to find a way to be alive. Nellie
Beatrice—the restless lasher-out—always referred to their resi-
dences as "Dead-and-Alive Holes": it's not too much to say that
John had more than a bit of her attitude in him. His version of
the raging, however, was witty, sardonic, and rhetorically height-
ened: he found images and flights of language to beat down the
enemy, show his superiority, and rise above them. Ironically the
Family Row was something that Osborne adapted in his own
life and work. Words are mostly fighting words, whether grim or
funny. Osborne seems to have elevated the dig and the insult to
the level of poetry. *A Better Class of Person*—the very title bites.
Or take the succinct description of Christmas with relatives: "It
was impossible not to be caught in some cross-fire or stray flack at
some points during these festive manoeuvres." Or take the family attitude toward John's new clothes: the trousers seemed "to
sprout pound-note signs all over them." Or John's description of
the dignity of age—"geriatric divinity." Or what the Groves and
the Osbornes had in common: "the heart pumped from birth by
misgiving." His plays are at their best when they prickle with the
intelligence of such lines.

The Osborne armory contains all kinds of variations of this
generalized pugnacity. They first developed in early boyhood

when he was at school in Ewell. A pal named Mickey Wall—one of those admirable pals that blokes have, like Amis's Wybrow or Larkin's Sutton—taught him a lot about fighting against the odds. Mickey had a characteristic way of annoying teachers without bringing down punishment on himself. He flapped his arms, talked in non sequiturs and spouted nonsense, refused to understand a reprimand. He threw victims off their game. Osborne goes so far as to describe the strategy as "Nietzschean Concentration of Will"; he wanted to be like the 9-year-old who could press buttons, yet maintain an "inability to be aroused." The two of them established the Viper Gang Club—"formed to strike," to *épater le bourgeois*. Osborne's "choler," however, was a part of his makeup that wasn't as whimsical and daft as Mickey's aggression. As a student in a very minor public school called St Michael's in *A Better Class of Person* (Belmont College in Devon)—where he was sent as a charity case after Dad's passing—he joined the boxing team and held his own. He was good at taking on a bully, even one who was a faculty member. After he struck a teacher who slapped him at a social function because he wouldn't turn off Frank Sinatra on the radio, his school career ended. It had been fairly humdrum: some Latin and French, some English classics including Dickens and Arnold, some guarded praise won for writing, some strong cider consumed at the local, some dreaming of looking up girls' tennis skirts and buying condoms that were never used. His ambition to attend Oxford was laughed at, and it's no surprise that he puts down the whole experience by calling the place "a fake public school," a "bargain basement education." Osborne liked the idea that even as a boy he could "smoke out" the phonies and the second-raters. He was proud of his talent to vex.

The other offensive weapon was an early and enduring love of voluptuousness and life freed from inhibitions. When dad was let go at the advertising agency in 1938—given a cheap "High Street clock" and a month's salary—he decided to take John and Nellie Beatrice to Margate for a week. In *A Better Class of Person* John evokes the scene: "When I first went to Las Vegas I immediately thought of those evenings in Margate and my parents, of fish and chips and Guinness. And streams of girls. I had never seen a chorus line before. As they tap-danced and swung their legs they would sing 'Lullaby of Broadway' and 'Shuffle Off to Buffalo,' which seemed to be that year's most popular show numbers." The seaside was the defining place in Osborne's erotic imagination (and it's interesting to note that he always kept a supply of naughty seaside postcards at the ready to write insulting notes on). The early Margate description is later echoed by this one about Brighton.

> As the word Brompton [where Dad was hospitalized] was to pain, Brighton was to pleasure. If I were to choose a way to die it would be after a drunken, fish-eating day ending up at the end of the Palace Pier. . . . No other resort has its simple raffishness. . . . It was still [in the early 1950s] the Mecca of the dirty weekend. . . . Brighton had randiness hanging in the air throughout the year. . . . Ozone in Eastbourne was spermatozoa in Brighton, burning brightly like little tadpoles of evening light across the front. Whenever I have lunch in Brighton, I always want to take someone to bed in the afternoon. To shudder one's last, thrusting, replete gasp between the sheets at 4 and 6 o'clock in Brighton, would be the most perfect last earthly delight.

Cheap and blowsy as this may be, it's a forceful assault on Grove–Osborne family wisdom like "Can't expect too much, go too far, only get disappointed." Osborne believed in something and went for it. He was conspicuous in his yellow pullover, jeered at by the local kids. As his young manhood opened out, he did whatever it took to defy the destiny awaiting most young men: a steady job, marriage, kiddies, aging. And he cultivated an unconventional manner without becoming a bohemian or an artiste: he found a mix of transgressiveness, sexual adventurism, literariness, and showbiz chaos to be the way out of Fulham and Stoneleigh.

Arnold Running, a foul-mouthed literary Canadian who edited a publication called *The Miller* (with articles about grinding grain), recognized young John's talents as an observer and writer—if not a natural born journalist. John was "cheeky"—which is to say spirited—but not pushy enough to be a first rate reporter. Running also didn't find John to be what we would call macho—found him a "panty-waist" (literally a child's two piece undergarment), a sissy. Elsewhere Osborne himself admits that he cultivated a campy, rather effeminate manner, so there may be some truth here; in any case the young man who liked to vex people was startled and amused by his boss's obscenity. He also took his advice: "You're too full of highbrow horse shit for Fleet Street. You better get rid of it somewhere else."

The next move would be to the theatre world, although there was a slight complication before he could escape. While working at *The Miller* and living with Nellie Beatrice, Osborne had become romantically involved with Renee Shippard, a very conventional and attractive girl he met at a dancing school. He had enrolled in the hope of being able to keep up with the Brylcreemed young fellows at the Victoria Inn, a local dance hall. Renee was from his suburban area, and they started spending every evening together, enjoying "snatched pelvic felicities during the Quickstep." One thing led to another and before long Renee got an engagement ring. But the trouble was the Shippards: "The front parlour gloom was the same I had known at Tottenham and Fulham, with the odour of anaemic self-righteousness, the lifeless whine, the lack of rigour or even gift of petty decision. Union with Renee soon appeared a consummation more devoutly to be escaped than contemplated." Meanwhile his dancing teacher's mother got him involved with an amateur dramatic group where he soon excelled in a production of *Blithe Spirit*. He delivered a wonderful imitation of the Rex Harrison part. From there it wasn't a great leap to a job as Assistant Stage Manager of a touring company which was offering a production of a war melodrama called *No Room at the Inn*.

The rest of the early struggle to be a theatre man is all about theatrical digs, northern beer, bad plays, late suppers, fights over playwrighting, "sleeping in till noon, feather beds, free films and fucks." Renee got her note of farewell, and John began his serious career as a womanizer. First with a winsome 22-year-old named Sheila, a controlling type who was the ingénue in the play; she spent off-time with him viewing cathedrals and (with some reluctance) went to bed. She was known in the company as "Miss Tight-arsed Bossy-drawers," and Osborne soon switched his affections to Stella Linden, the wife of a gay theatrical entrepreneur whom he worked for in London. She was a powerful woman ("with a pelvic arch like the skull of an ox") who was influential in getting him started as a writer, brought out his fighting side, and made him a proud sexual performer. He bought a pair of ridiculously expensive yellow silk pajamas in Simpson's for their first night (is this the yellow of Aubrey Beardsley or just a grown up version of the sweater?) and made love to her nine times a day when they were together. She tore one of his first plays to shreds, told him he knew nothing of playmaking, advised him to read Pinero to learn craft, and then collaborated with him—actually helped him to revise the failed effort. She juiced up his work, made it more commercial. In his autobiography he balks at the lessons: even as a young man he knew she was cheap as a writer, strove for easy effect, and wanted a play to be about nice people an audience could identify with. Stella wouldn't write a play with "Viper Gang jeers"—and that's what constituted theatre for the young Osborne. He wanted to appeal to a "captive minority audience"—people who got angry, were moved deeply, and for whom "walking out" was something that might even be enjoyed. But he lived in a time when "There was nothing like a dame and an unlovable dame was nothing." This was the late 1940s when as edgy as you could get in the theatre was Noel Coward's devil-may-care. Osborne wanted to say damn you—and his first play of worth, *Epitaph for George Dillon*, had a terribly wrong word in the title.

The Osborne aesthetic—if that's not too highfalutin a term—was a combination of elements: passionate language, unpleasant things, pleasurable release as a gauge of significance, and transgression everywhere. His theatrical beau ideal was the music hall star Max Miller, a performer who had most of what Osborne strove for—minus, perhaps the passionate language. Max was the hit of the Holborn Empire in the 1940s. Osborne had seen him perform twice and admired his "flashiness." By this he meant "The common, cheap and mean parodied and seized on as a style of life in face of the world's dullards." Max wore an outrageous blue silk suit and talked "supercharged filth"—yet no one could lock him up. "He appeared to live in pubs, digs, race-course and theatre bars." His method—and elsewhere Osborne identifies it in Nietzsche—is danger. His subject matter is, mostly, girls. "Unwilling girls, give-her-a-shilling-and-she'll-be-willing girls, Annie and Fanny, girls who hadn't found out, girls on their honeymoon, fan dancers minus their fans, pregnant girls and barmaids the stork put the wind up every six weeks." Osborne would use Max's crudity and jolly awfulness for their own sake—for shock value—but also for the sake of ridiculing the limited, coarse, mean-spirited parts of the Brit sensibility: when he used this material in *The Entertainer*, he meant to let his audience see what they were.

The making of Osborne the artist and personality involved a lot of drudgery as well. The late 1940s and 1950s up to his triumphant year of 1956 were not exactly a period of unqualified success. John moved from one seedy situation to another. When down in Brighton with Stella, he had to turn to being a washer-up at a hotel that catered to Pinewood film people. He saw a whole contorted vision of life in the kitchen—and later in *A Better Class of Person* quoted Arnold Wesker, a Marxist-oriented delineator of life among the strugglers. In Wesker's best-known play *The Kitchen*, everyone wants to fight everyone else in order to assert manhood. "Listen, you put a man in the plate room all day, he's got dishes to make clean and stinking bins to take away and floors to sweep, what else is there for him to do—he wants to fight." This was certainly a large part of what was on Osborne's mind. Soon he went to work for the Saga Repertory Company and became friends with its artistic director Anthony Creighton—down the road they would collaborate. In the meantime he acted in such dreadful plays as *Duet for Two Hands*, about a pianist who loses his hands and has a murderer's grafted on—with predictable results. He was the Prince in a ludicrously overacted *Hamlet*, exulting in misogyny and lunging at his fellow actors (fueled by whisky, of course). "Seldom can a Hamlet have exemplified so wholeheartedly the vices mocked in the speech to the Players." At another theatre company based in Bridgewater, Osborne played the part of a fellow taking some liberties with a housemaid; Pamela Lane played the young girl—and soon she was Osborne's new love, not to mention the model for Alison in *Look Back in Anger*.

Pamela Lane was a graduate of RADA and quite a striking presence; her close cropped auburn hair, her huge green eyes (which seemed to plead and mock), and her obvious superiority to the run-of-the-mill types in provincial theatre made her just right for the attentions of a young man escaping a dreary past. Osborne's biographer John Heilpern quotes the young lover's list of powerful redheads—Borgia, Beatrice, among them—and offers the kicker line: "A redheaded Doris Day was unthinkable." Another strong woman like Stella, Pamela had better taste in writing and was classier. She used the expression "D and B" (dull and boring) on Osborne's draft of *Look Back in Anger*—and he was determined not to be that. He was also intent upon marrying her, which he did against the wishes of her parents. The Lanes were on the border line of gentility, Mr. Lane's father having been a master draper; yet their social position was complicated by the fact that Lane had been a flying ace in the Great War and a hero. "Mummy" was a self-important battleaxe who couldn't stand John from the first, principally because he was a little nobody who pressed provincial buttons by acting in a campy manner. Heilpern puts it well: "Osborne's idea of an actor was to act one." The couple was married by a local vicar at 8 o'clock in the morning—with only the parents in attendance; they thereafter had a full day of acting, with time out for a grim wedding luncheon at an establishment for "Masons and Rotarians" (as Osborne snidely put it).

The ingredients of *Look Back in Anger*—rage, class resentment, sadism, self-pity, boredom—are pretty much the stuff of Osborne's life. But they didn't come together in an artistic form for a while. Osborne and Creighton had remained friends and when the young couple came to London—Bridgewater being a little uncomfortable for free spirits—they wound up spending a period sharing Creighton's digs in Hammersmith. That didn't last long because Pamela got a lead part in Derby. John was also diverted from his writing by a job in Kidderminster. And then Pamela started to carry on with a dentist. John went back to stage managing—and even had to do his Christmas stint at the GPO to make ends meet. But in the year 1954, he was writing again— with Creighton as his collaborator; they dashed off a play on the McCarthy hearings and went on to *Epitaph for George Dillon*. It's a play about the suburbs, about the hopeless struggle to be an artist in a cheesy culture. It has a hustler agent who wants a young playwright to dirty up a script.

But it was only on his next try, with *Look Back in Anger*, that Osborne broke through, found his audience, and created his bloke persona in the character of Jimmy Porter. John had been Jimmy for years, of course—frustrated, rebellious, more than a bit nasty, too heavy for the lightweights in school, in the theatre, in his own daily life. In a string of plays—*The Entertainer, Luther, Inadmissible Evidence*—he creates other versions of his first great protagonist, variations on the theme of himself, imaginative renderings of his own struggle to be a man. He also acted out in real life, doing the obnoxious, over-the-top things that Jimmy and the others did. He was a loudmouth like Jimmy, hectoring people for his entire life. He enjoyed trash talk, "supercharged filth" like Archie Rice in *The Entertainer*. He butted heads with authority—not the Church but the literary and critical establishment. And he made a mess of domesticity, fatherhood, friendships, personal health—like Bill Maitland in *Inadmissible Evidence* he wound up letting the chaos come. No wonder he ironically titled his second volume of autobiography *Almost a Gentleman*—he knew that despite the money, country houses, the Aston-Martin, the hols in the South of France, culture, champagne, Turnbull and Asser clothes he wasn't the real thing. Just didn't have the self-control and dignity for it.

The noise all started in 1956, the only real date in British theatre history, according to one critic. *Look Back in Anger* was not a true overnight hit, having collected some pretty indifferent and hostile reviews in the dailies. But the Sunday papers made Osborne's play a phenomenon. The powerful critic Kenneth Tynan took the play personally and said he couldn't love anyone who didn't embrace it. He was heartened by Jimmy Porter's lack of good taste and by his emotional vitality. Yes, his response was probably a minority view—confined to the over six million Brits between 20 and 30 years old. Tynan, an Establishment figure who would specialize in insulting the Establishment, was just the right defender for Osborne; but John's nastiness and bad taste were much stronger than his sense of indebtedness. By the year 1973, he was accusing Tynan of "intellectual spivvery" and of being a "disastrous influence."

And Jimmy Porter is the same, a character whose major allegiance is to his own sensibility, his own pain, his own collection of pleasures and grievances. Bloke life is by and large not political—unless you think in terms of a party of one, or of being, as Osborne would put it in one of his titles, "a patriot for me." Jimmy is largely concerned with what we today would call being in touch with your feelings—he is the grandfather of being in touch. He's determined to dredge up bad memories, injurious impressions of others, off-the-cuff social observations—in short, most of what we edit out of civilized intercourse. He's in touch with what we usually don't want to touch—and the major theme is pain. Most British people restrain the impulse to exhibit their own pain and inflict it openly on others; most British people are too nice to give pain—to insult others openly. That's what manners are for—the control of aggression. A gentleman, as Newman told us, is someone who doesn't inflict pain. But Osborne's Jimmy does it during an entire play: like some kind of reverse Utilitarian, he thinks the well-lived life consists of confronting pain and avoiding pleasure. (Shades of the Grove Family Repertory Company.) Osborne's essayistic profile of Jimmy in the script—a kind of cheating for a playwright—tells us that he is "a disconcerting mixture of sincerity and cheerful malice, tenderness and freebooting cruelty." Jimmy uses music hall skits, one-liners, silly poetry, acting out, trumpet playing, and plain old-fashioned mauling to get at other people's vulnerabilities and expose his own. He is, as high-toned Helena puts it, a tiresome young man.

He tires you out with his favorite subject—England's deadness. It's Sunday in *Look Back In Anger*—the day lashed and bashed by Dickens in *Little Dorrit* and by Penelope Gilliatt (Osborne's third wife) in the screenplay "Sunday, Bloody Sunday." Dickens's Arthur Clennam endured the joylessness, the maddening bells, the desolation of the streets; Gilliatt's young woman felt that soul-sinking sensation that comes from love denied. Jimmy's pronouncement identifies the 1950s version of the problem: dead drift, with those same old bells. "Nobody cares . . . No beliefs, no convictions, no enthusiasm." The play is almost a game—let's get in touch with something, even something ugly. Awareness is the object—of family, customs, one's own impulses, and (but not usually in this play) the joy of being alive.

Jimmy—"sensitive to the point of vulgarity"—is the twentieth-century man of feeling. He goes to work making us aware of how tepid and self-protective bourgeois Brits have become. The

basic situation involves a lower middle-class young man, his genteel wife and her parents (and off-stage brother Nigel), the young
man's pal Cliff, the wife's elegant girlfriend Helena: the gritty
and the genteel face off. Osborne gets fights going in order to
expose what England is made of: to him it's not so much snobbery and underdog victimhood; it's on one hand the "sycophan-
tic, phlegmatic and pusillanimous" people in Alison's camp versus
the spirited, suffering people in Jimmy's. The first are no longer
capable of lordly status assertion: they rule by understatement and
convention, the national tolerance for inertia, by retreating into
the "sanctuary" of their own stupidity when change or improve-
ment is proposed. Alison's brother Nigel, according to Jimmy, will
one day be a Cabinet minister, not because he's hard-driving but
because "somewhere in the back of that mind is the vague knowledge that he and his pals have been plundering and fooling everybody for generations." He's "a chinless wonder from Sandhurst"
who should get a medal for being vague and hazy about most
things—especially about knowledge of ordinary human beings.
"For Vaguery in the Field," Jimmy says. The phrase is almost like
Dickens's "How Not To Do It"—the motto of the nineteenth-
century administrative class. For Osborne it's how not to see the
point of anything vital and intense.

Jimmy's attacks are brilliant flailing rather than reformist rhetoric. His very appearance makes him into a frenzied demi-god
from the lower orders. Alison married him because "Everything
about him seemed to burn, his face, the edges of his hair glis-
tened and seemed to spring off his head, and his eyes were so
blue and full of the sun." He has the magnetism of a jazz trumpet man who once had his own band, the intelligence of a university graduate who can toss off witty lines about T. S. Eliot,
the careless appeal of a fellow who would rather run a sweet-stall
than take the regular deadening job available to the educated but
unprivileged Brit. Marriage to Alison is a screwed up mix of verbal abuse, sex, and sentimentality. He berates her daily, especially

on this typical Sunday as she stands ironing: she takes his tongue lashing—about class, her family, her own lack of grit—and seems to understand that he's suffering. Actually that property of his nature is all he has left, according to her. At one point he causes her to be burned by the iron. He calls her "that cruel, stupid girl" after he hears she's going to have his baby. He's quite proud of not being a gentleman and of being perfectly capable of hitting a woman. The awfulness of Jimmy the husband is topped off by the game of bears and squirrels—the first protective, the second cute and none-too-bright and "great eyed" like Pamela Lane. The complication is that Jimmy finds Alison like a devouring python— passive aggressive. This isn't to say she's like her bullying mummy (compared to a rhino, a matelow, a night in a Bombay brothel); she is winsome, tall and dark, with delicate features and an elegance that's apparent even when wearing a "grubby skirt" and one of Jimmy's shirts. But she's dangerous. (Comic misogyny is a feature of the play—Jimmy and Cliff's lyrics, composed when they're loafing about, being most notable: "She said she was called a little Gidding, but she was more like a gelding iron!") Numbers of critics have said that Jimmy's abusiveness is reminiscent of Stanley Kowalski's; meanwhile, Alison's charms and refinement are powerful. She clings like Tennessee Williams's Stella—and returns to him at the end of the play after a period of separation.

But the similarities should not make us forget that Jimmy is more than brute maleness: he's a social philosopher without credentials, stuck at a sweet-stall, and determined to leave his imprint on life, have his say. Surely part of his problem is described by Harvey Mansfield when he refers to "unemployed manliness": there's no war, no brave cause, no heroic deeds to be performed. Jimmy plainly says that he has no world of his own; he's in worse shape than Alison's father—once a military man who led a Maharaja's army; even though the old man is superannuated, he has his memories: "All homemade cakes, croquet, bright ideas and bright uniforms. Always the same picture: high summer, the long days in the sun, slim volumes of verse, crisp linen, the smell of starch." Jimmy appears to have nothing but anger—he's never been part of brave causes and the sweet life of the gentlefolk who fought them. (Let's not get into the fact that he talks out of both sides of his mouth, showing affection for the old Edwardian good life and contempt for its clueless descendants like brother Nigel.) And in the 1950s even that precious commodity suffering is muted by false ideas of progress and rhetoric about equal opportunity. About the only thing left for Jimmy is raging. Like Osborne—who would write a screed to the Tribune in 1961 called "Damn You, England"—Jimmy can damn his countrymen, their lack of moral magnitude. Everything has grown small. "If the big bang does come, and we all get killed off, it won't be in aid of the old-fashioned, grand design. . . . About as pointless and inglorious as stepping in front of a bus." What's a poor bloke to do?

Jimmy's last stand is a defense of something he's deficient in—decent humanity. And the occasion for his humane speechmaking is the suffering of two ordinary people—a character modeled exactly on Osborne's father and an old woman whom he knew from boyhood, the mother of his friend Hugh. As a little boy Jimmy watched his father die: it's the defining experience of his childhood, the event that made him human. "The family hoped he'd [Jimmy's father would] get on with it, without too much vulgar fuss." But Jimmy sat and listened to the man's stories of the Spanish Civil War—and cared. "Anyone who's never watched somebody die is suffering from a pretty bad case of virginity," Jimmy blurts out to Helena. His rant against Alison, delivered to her friend Helena later in the play, is caused by an identical failure of human sympathy: his wife has not risen to the challenge of feeling the pain of a dying person. The old woman who gave Jimmy his start-up money for the sweet stall has just passed and Jimmy is again facing the death of a loved one alone. Of Alison he says, "She thought that because Hugh's mother was a deprived and ignorant old woman, who said all the wrong things in all the wrong places, she couldn't be taken seriously." A "muffled cry of despair" escapes from Jimmy as he gets slapped by Helena for his hysteria and venom; but no sooner does she see the whole package of bloke tenderness and meanness—including I don't care if it [Alison's baby] has two heads!—than she follows the slap with a passionate kiss. This caring Brit Kowalski is attractive because of his suffering. His "burning virility of mind and spirit" can face pain boldly. As a matter of fact, in a screwed-up way, it yearns for power in others—the strength to face pain; it also yearns for pity and companionship. And in a contradictory, screwed-up way, it yearns for people to "splash about" in the pain of existence.

Jimmy's feelings are made into something portentous in the play. Helena says he's born out of his time: "I feel he thinks he's in the middle of the French Revolution," she says. He's living in the iron age of the Cold War and mummy and daddy and a proper routine and post-war letdown when he has the fiery soul of a warrior. His war of course is waged against the national numbness: "They all want to escape the pain of being alive." "They" want to avoid "messing up" their "nice clean soul." The cleanliness is likened to saintliness but it also sounds a good deal like honor—that old-fashioned stuff that makes you a gentleman. If you insist on it "you'll never make it as a human being."

Osborne certainly lived by the code of messiness. He soon married Mary Ure, the leading lady who played Alison. She was a Scots beauty from a middle-class family who wanted children; never a first-ranked actress she had her moments in the sun, including exciting times when *Look Back* went to New York for a run. The couple was in the papers constantly—on the town, marching for disarmament. She looked great on stage in Jimmy's shirt—or sipping champagne with John. But he was, by his own admission, "squalid" in his dealings with her. As a baby was about to be born, he was carrying on with a Swiss hooker named Francine Brandt, finishing an affair with set designer Jocelyn Rickards, and getting very serious about film critic Penelope Gilliatt. The tabloids noted that daddy was "SHY" when Ure delivered. But was he daddy? Or was the father actor Robert Shaw? The whole thing was perfect for a playwright who loved the theme of betrayal and intimacy that turns to pain. The highly intellectual Gilliatt, a major film critic and later on a screenwriter, was his next fiery redhead. Although wild by nature—she was to become "fucking friends" with Edmund Wilson and Mike Nichols—she also had a domestic side, loved a beautiful home and lifestyle, and wanted a child by Osborne. Nolan, born in 1965, was the product of their 3-year marriage. For a good while they were a loving couple; Gilliatt was a very affectionate woman; they shared their passionate natures, love of fun, drink, and pet names (they both were known as Banks). But Osborne had his eye on actress Jill Bennett, star of his play *A Patriot for Me*. She was a hard-drinking, drug-taking standard bearer for swinging London—the glam, the diva routine, the scene making, the suicide attempts. They were married for 8 years. Osborne came to hate her and didn't mind savaging her in his autobiography *Almost a Gentleman*, that is after she committed suicide and there was no danger of a libel suit. Osborne settled into a fifth marriage with journalist Helen Dawson, a balanced and devoted woman who evidently managed to control a chronic womanizer. What she couldn't do, however, was control Osborne's temper and extravagance. The former led him to throw his only child out of his country house as a teenager; never having been a teen himself—the young person of his era was not the center of media attraction and the marketing industry—he didn't know how to handle the self-absorption, moodiness, and bad musical tastes of Nolan. He found her to be terminally selfish, conformist—and with that he dismissed her from his life. This of course is Jimmy raging against people who don't care—but the stakes were higher than in a stage play.

Meanwhile, John Osborne was becoming one of the spendthrift writers of his age. The epic tale of a bloke and his money—fabulous sums made and squandered (the screenplay for *Tom Jones* made him a multimillionaire), country houses, cars, and champagne right up to the brink of insolvency—reminds one of F. Scott Fitzgerald. The "Welsh upstart from Fulham" (as Jill Bennett called him) had his own film company with Tony Richardson, lolled poolside in Hollywood with celebrities Vivian Leigh, Marilyn Monroe, and Simone Signoret, sneered at the mob from his Bentley—and died while in residence at his country house The Hurst in Shropshire near the Welsh border. John Heilpern tells us that his debts totaled £377,000. He had been hounded for years by creditors, but hung on as a squire, even a serious Anglican. Always showy—from his days with the yellow pullover—he was almost a gentleman in appearance, the cloth cap perhaps giving him away.

Osborne's early run as a playwright is one of the triumphs of the bloke sensibility in English literary culture. He quickly followed *Look Back in Anger* with another strike at conventional decency, good manners, and restraint. Archie Rice in *The Entertainer*—despite his shop-worn gags—lives up to the play's title: he's startling and stimulating, not as tiresome and sententious as Jimmy. The play opened in 1957, the year after the Suez crisis, and it's a microcosm of England's troubles: failure of big plans, showiness without substance, the old class system displaying itself, and humiliation. Anthony Eden, the Prime Minister, got England in over its head by trying to stop Nasser's seizure of the Suez Canal. He didn't understand the times he was living in—everything from Arab nationalism to U.S. strategy. Archie for his part has it in mind to give the public a great show—and he too can't accept that the times have changed. It's the dawn of rock 'n' roll, that killer of music hall routines. Yet Archie still uses the cheeky manner of Max Miller, the sexy-corny jokes, the comic deflation (he's played "in front of them all 'The Queen,' 'The Duke of Edinburgh,' 'The Prince of Wales,' and the—what's the name of the other pub.") He'll have nothing to do with "drab equality"—and in his own way thinks of himself as a superior sort; landladies love Archie, considering him "obviously such a gentleman." And it should be remembered that he's the product of a minor public day school in London, the kind of place that "managed to produce some raffish middle-class adventurers as well as bank managers and a poet." Yet the play is about the big flop of Archie's career, family fights, the mortifying contrast between Archie and his successful barrister brother Bill, the pathetic death of Archie's father Billy (a performer on his last legs) and most tragically the death of Archie's son Mick in the Suez campaign. Archie's wife Phoebe, a whiner like Nellie Beatrice, puts the situation this way: "He always builds everything up. And it never turns out." For Archie his money troubles and the taxman mean escape to Canada or jail. His last routine is a song with the lyric "Why should I care, / Why should I let it touch me." The "bloke at the side here with a hook"—almost like Eisenhower pulling the rug from under Eden's brave adventure—is about to end Archie's act, but Archie goes on anyway—offering the cheeky challenge to the audience which Osborne's tombstone has carved on it: "Let me know where you're working tomorrow night—and I'll come and see YOU." In *The Uses of Literacy* social critic Richard Hoggart marvelously captures the spirit of media loudmouths who are just like Archie: "We will pay handsomely that man who gives some release to our sense of inferiority and disillusion by expressing himself violently in print on what we all hate." In Archie's case his nastiness and aggression are meant to play to the audience. "Did I tell you about the wife?" is the most predictable sort of cheap joke. Snarling against the National Health, championing "number one" against "drab equality," sounding off about militarism, bragging about being moderate and normal in his sexual appetites—sad to say these are the staples of his act.

This play about failure is not without its moments of transcendence. True, Archie is awful: he's cheating on his sad-sack wife, ready to use his old father for his own publicity stunt; he's a condescending, sneering, nasty scamp who ridicules Phoebe in his act (a "moron glacee"), has fun with cheap homophobia ("I'm normal"), and tells his family off for their mediocrity ("We don't ever succeed in anything") when he's the quintessence of mediocrity. But he's at war with himself, knows that he can't feel deeply: he gets back at his own emotional numbness by admitting that there's something great in this world—the joyous, intense outburst of creativity. He once heard it in the voice of a fat Negro woman singing her heart out in an American bar: "If I'd done one thing in my life as good as that I'd have been all right." It's better than British stiff-upper-lip carrying on without a fuss, better than Trafalgar Square rallies. It's caring transformed into art. Archie, let it be said, knows it when he hears it. And to this reader and appreciator of Osborne's characters, Archie's final scene has the same quality. The horrible compromiser—half bloke, "the same as you out there," half sneering gent—becomes fully human.

But that isn't to say that the drama's humane moments cancel the general sleaziness. "Land of Hope and Glory" plays as we see "a nude in Britannia's helmet and holding a bulldog and trident" on a gauze screen. Nostalgia and cynicism are hard to separate out. Osborne tells us that "the music hall is dying and, with it, a significant part of England." Its folk art is soon to be displaced by the rock 'n' roll industry; but in music hall the authentic always consorts with the lowdown, British pride and fellow feeling get mixed up with cheapness. And that's the life that Osborne led. At his memorial service Michael Ball sang the old music hall favorite: "If you were the only girl in the world," and the friends and admirers sang along, doubtless unable to forget the rakehell they were singing in honor of. Osborne was always an edgy, ambiguous figure and a creator of figures who combined awfulness and yearning. Jimmy and Archie were just the beginning.

He gave the public a jolt when he turned to historical drama in *Luther*, but that didn't mean he was abandoning his mission to rage. The play took time out from beating up on the English character, but it still was about rebellion and the restless soul of a modern man. Martin Luther couldn't stand late medieval routine any more than Jimmy could stand the English Sunday. The new play had a hero butting heads with indulgence salesmen, prelates and a very pretentious Pope—very powerful and authoritarian figures; Jimmy had opponents like Mummy and Daddy and Nigel—less important but still insidious people. *Luther* and *Look Back* were both about forming a conscience, *The Entertainer* being about the inability to do so. Osborne's vision of a man's power went back and forth during the 1950s and early 1960s—*Epitaph* is about selling out; *Look Back* about standing up; *The Entertainer* is about collapsing; *Luther* is again about standing up; *Inadmissible Evidence* is about total meltdown and loss of identity.

Manliness is fully employed in *Luther*: the causes to embrace are Scripture, conscience, and grace. And Martin, unlike Jimmy, is not battling vagueness—there's vivid mumbo jumbo in place of the plain words of the Bible, false relics for sale, slimy characters in high places, gross ecclesiastical extravagance. There's plenty for a well-educated fellow from a humble background to do if he wants to make a better world. Or as Martin puts it to Father Staupitz, his superior in the Augustinian order, "have you ever felt humiliated to find that you belong to a world that's dying?" The way out of humiliation—proud assertion—is actually the driving idea of the play. And Martin's assertions are almost always impolite. In order to have his say, he has to talk about farting and shitting, nose bleeds, withered arms, infections, and cauterization. "If I break wind in Wittenberg, they might smell it in Rome," Martin says. Warned by Staupitz to be prudent, he replies that he can't be any such thing: he's the type who must talk about "pigs and Christ in the same breath." Or take this one about the three ways of escaping despair: to have faith in Christ, "to become enraged by the world and make its nose bleed, and the third is the love of a woman."

Ridicule, invective, and self-laceration are the responses to the awfulness of human nature and human institutions. Luther's over-stimulated conscience goes to work on evils within himself and in the Church. One wonderful flight of language—a swipe at the monastery—has Luther declaring that there's nothing to be gained from the religious life. He sees himself as still envious, impatient, passionate—"I'm living in the Devil's worm-bag." One of the Proverbs torments him: "Know thou the state of thy flocks." This is the same idea that possesses Jimmy on a Sunday evening: what is the spiritual state of one's countrymen? In fact the flocks are busy bargaining with God: medieval religious practice, says Luther, is all about getting the best deal through indulgences, the possession of relics, and ritual. Martin tells a hilarious story about a man being forgiven in advance for sins he intended to commit. The only way out of such cagey Christianity is grace. In this play grace is the be all and end all of the spiritual life: it's the sixteenth century antidote to despair, just as strong feeling is the twentieth century cure. Letting grace into your life is as wrenching for Luther as dredging up feeling is for Jimmy. These men come alive when they are in pain. Staupitz tells Martin that a man with a strong sword will draw it sometime, "even if it's only to turn it on himself." This power to wound is crucial in Osborne's life and work.

Inadmissible Evidence is Osborne's darkest presentation of the bloke's fate: the aggression at work throughout the play is not cathartic; there are no breakthrough insights, no glimpses of joy. Osborne's character Bill Maitland is stuck with his own nature—mediocre, lustful, and selfish. What gives the play its excitement is the spectacle of one man able to see so much about himself, even to the extent of predicting his own desperate future. Maitland, a 31-year-old London solicitor, is on trial, as it were: in a dreamy set of scenes he is accused of not having led a good life. The judge is himself, and the proceedings have the flavor of Tolstoy's Ivan Ilych looking at his own falseness over a long span of time. Bill's nothing much as a lawyer, only tolerably bright, not in the league with the Oxbridge types. He has no friends—only a clerk who's looking to move to a different firm. He's having Osborne's problems with his women. He's cheating on his wife with Liz, a civilized woman who has had it with Bill's failure to be a man of real passion and devotion; he's even cheating on Liz with his secretary Joy, a sweet young thing who diverts him from his inner torment. That torment has to do with self-doubt, lost chances, and a bad character. It's an anguish— Dostoyevskian in its lacerating self-hatred when its not Tolstoyan in its ironic self-exposure—that spreads across his whole life: "I myself am more packed with spite and twitching with revenge than anyone I know of." But unlike Jimmy Porter's pain, this is the stuff of guilt, nothing to be proud of. Maitland feels sorry for no one but himself, doesn't even have Archie Rice's compassion and admiration for the black singer, doesn't quite care if others are suffering. In a self-fulfilling prophecy of his horrible dealings with Nolan, Osborne has Bill speak of his teenage daughter with cold contempt: she's a squalid kid, swinging and cool and unloving. Why not tell her off and brush her off?

As usual with Osborne it's difficult to know where irony ends and sincere nastiness begins: Bill Maitland is certainly held up for our inspection but he's also allowed to be a spokesman for his truths. They include things that we can't help but see in his way, even though they're so unpleasant. Take Bill on "a nice serious fellow": "That just about sounds like every supine, cautious young husband, all about six degrees under the proper consciousness in the land." Or take his view of Brits during the holidays: they "are the people who go up every year like it was holy communion to have a look at the Christmas decorations in Regent Street." Or Bill on girls before the age of cool teens like his daughter: "their sweety tacky lipsticks and silk stockings on coupons and permanent waves and thick hipped heavy skirts."

Bill's clearest look at himself is a summation of the Osborne battle against his time, his nature, and his country: "I haven't ever been made to feel sharp or with it or representative of any damn thing."

5

KENNETH TYNAN

Kenneth Tynan—critic, essayist, and all round man of the theater—was once the premier literary-cultural bloke in England, the brilliantly aggressive personality who was famous for shocking the public with his opinions and language, exhibiting his capacity for self-possession and domination, parlaying his wit and intelligence into one of the most intense social existences of the age, being a sexual adventurer and spokesman for sexual experiment. Kingsley Amis and John Osborne were womanizers, drinkers, self-aggrandizers, and loud mouths; but Tynan refined the act and took it to new heights. He was a phenomenon of the sensual life, a kind of philosopher of new sensations, immediate experiences, and daring things. He responded to plays, books, ideas, food, sport, and beautiful women in a richer and more complex way than his contemporaries. He seemed to realize the full potential of bloke life.

From the start he was a star—never an underpaid librarian like Larkin, a teacher with a load of student papers like Amis, or an assistant stage manager and postal worker like Osborne. He plunged headlong into English intellectual life, the theatre, glamorous romance. He was instantly at home in the great world, having never given a thought to any other place. He never passed through the lowlands of early failure and apprenticeship.

He seemed to live the central fantasy of the bloke: making it all go your way. As a boy in King Edward's School in Birmingham, he wrote an essay called "Insignificance": it dilated on the fear that we have described earlier—being no one in particular, never being noticed, feeling the downward pull of dreary English life. While young Ken articulated something he would never have to worry about, he also stated the conflict of his life—the struggle and exhilaration of keeping his persona and his work high-powered and important to his contemporaries.

Tynan was a 6-year-old marvel—writing plays and astonishing his family with his intelligence. But that didn't mean there were no shadows and obstacles. He was the illegitimate son of Sir Peter Peacock, a fact he didn't confront until his father's death. Sir Peter was one of those late Victorian business phenomena, a shoe-maker's son who rose from abject poverty to wealth, civic prominence, and a knighthood. Peter's elder brother Albert got his siblings into the covered market at Warrington selling matches, shoe polish, and toys; the boys then founded a chain of penny bazaars—and their cheap and garish shops sprung up all over England. Peter subsequently went into the coal and contracting business, founded an accounting firm, and became mayor of Warrington six times. He married and had a family—but also had another secret family with Rose Tynan in Birmingham. Rose, a volunteer postal worker during the Great War, was a working-class girl whom he met at a whist drive when he was mayor. Kenneth was "Mr. Tynan's" son, which is to say a bit of a fabrication from the beginning. Mr. Tynan was supposedly—according to Ken's birth certificate of 1927—a draper; actually he was a showy man with a diamond ring, swallow-tailed coat, and Daimler. Kenneth Tynan's biographer Kathleen, his second wife, called Peter a "thrusting" man. Like Sydney Larkin, he was not to be confused with refined middle-class gentlemen; he was a rough and ready success. Drive, nerve, desire to dominate—and a high tolerance for the risk involved—were also the traits of Kenneth.

Kenneth was a stammerer, a problem that Kathleen connects with his lifelong desire to be heard: "if anyone tried to inhibit that extravagance of opinion or expression he would push it even further. Throughout his life he refused to be moderate or merely reasonable." His specialty was imposing his opinions, assuming the role of leader and tastemaker. "Aren't you following me?" was one of his lines. He evaluated his parents' taste in domestic appointments—glass vases and paintings of cows—and turned the awful paintings to the wall. On the wall of his own room were pictures of Humphrey Bogart, Peter Lorre, and Peggy Cummins (lead player in the loopy noir "Gun Crazy").

At King Edward VI Grammar School in Birmingham Ken was in his element. The place was famous for competing with Eton and Harrow for scholarships to university, for its tolerant egalitarianism, and for offering a superb classical humanist education. Ken published reviews in the school *Chronicle*, some of the material even finding its way into his first book, *He That Plays the King*. He knew from those days that he was a critic, not a poet or story teller, but he also knew that the essayist's eloquence and love of evoking and convincing were part of literature. He debated as well and had his maiden voyage as an outrageous figure by opposing the motion that "This House Thinks the Present Generation Has Lost the Ability to Entertain Itself." He argued for the enduring pleasures of masturbation. He also startled his peers and teachers with all the new films and books and plays he discovered. He lectured on Eisenstein, touted *New Yorker* writers, and was an Orson Welles champion. Of the latter he wrote, "Orson Welles is a self-made man and how he loves his Maker." Ken had a "new pose": "arrogance, bass voice, hanging lower lip." He loved "Whoreson Welles"—and would come to know his idol. But meanwhile he was dashing to London at 15, getting to know the people at Ealing Studios, the bookstalls, cheap restaurants, and amusement arcades.

The street life of Birmingham also had its charms, mostly female. One girl, "a light heavyweight," "kissed like a kick from Whirlaway." Ken lost his virginity in a doorway to a "despicable hoyden" named Enid, a blond who was another fierce kisser. On a more elevated level he romanced a young actress named Pauline Whittle, one of the featured players in a local dramatic society. She was 2 years older, a soulful dark-haired beauty who worshipped his already polished, witty style and prepossessing figure. They were boyfriend and girlfriend. Meanwhile he had snagged the part of Hamlet in the company's production. He also held court at a coffee shop named Kardomah, cut a dandiacal figure, and put in long hours in the local public library. Studious and streetwise, he seemed never to let up or let his audience down.

Like Welles, Ken loved his Maker and orchestrated a series of campaigns to make him famous. He lectured on "ART AND I . . . a history of the Influences that have gone to the making of KPT." He wore a check ladies' raincoat to a football match. And he topped off his school career by organizing a conference attended by London theatre critic James Agate. This was a splash which included his Hamlet performance, a chamber concert, a screening of "Citizen Kane," a cricket match, and a dance. Ken was the impresario—and soon was on friendly terms with Agate, going up to London, lunching at Café Royal, and receiving praise for his essays from the 68-year-old writer. He was told to make his own style, make the reader say "That's Tynan." But he was also warned about trying to develop too many ideas at once, being overly rich and eager to say it all.

Tynan was that golden kind of schoolboy who swung between extracurricular glory and academic excellence: enviable worldly achievement and perfect schoolwork. He went on to one of the most glamorous Oxford colleges, Magdalen; even though his father was very comfortable, he had a "demyship," (peculiar to his college and worth £fifty), a City of Birmingham scholarship, and a state scholarship. He traveled to the university in his father's

Daimler, with his mother, Pauline, and a couple of lemon tea cakes that Rose had supplied: he was cutting a figure, but there was a touch of provincial homeboy, something not county and posh. (Sean Puffy Combs, as he contemplated buying up London theatres, expressed his admiration for homeboy Tynan's transgressive style.) Tynan claimed to have found his identity and his spiritual home at Oxford, but there was ruefulness in his voice as he threw aside awful Birmingham. Oxford removed something from him "and replaced it with a Rolls-Royce spare part . . . I gained speed and sophistication." But he claimed not to know quite what he lost. This observer of his life can only say that knowing you lost something is the main thing: it shows that Tynan couldn't fool himself, couldn't forget the paintings of cows, the ugliest city in Europe, and the middle-class flavor of his boyhood.

Oxford—one of the biggest academic playing fields in the world—did not daunt young Tynan. Besides having arrived in a Daimler rather than the local butcher's car (recall Amis), he arrived with just the right amount of confidence, achievement, and sophistication. He started, as it were, as a finished product—not a resistor, a clod, an oddball, or a ruffian. Brilliance and glamour were always in long supply at the University, but this undergraduate's mark was soon everywhere. His tutor C. S. Lewis, renowned for his scholarship and literary distinction, took to the boy from Birmingham and his prose. He thought that Ken's essays were like what Lamb and Gibbon would have produced as young men had they been the same person—which is to say a sharp, vital, intense kind of prose. Tynan's interests were broad, not at all confined to the contemporary scene so favored by most undergraduates. The medieval mind and Milton were very important elements in his development. He loved the classics that Larkin and Amis loathed, but they got the Firsts and Tynan got his Second.

Tynan—be it said—made the extracurricular life into a career; to Amis and Larkin it was a pastime, a relief, a raucous protest. But Ken was made for the place—for all its wanton possibility and intellectual excitement—and knew it. Kathleen says he "took possession of Oxford," and his activities—editorships of magazines, writing, acting, debating at the Union, party throwing, seducing young women and proposing marriage (repeatedly), dressing in a plum doeskin suit, showboating and living large on a moderate allowance—prove the point. True, Oxford was not what it had been in the 1920s in terms of glamour; but Tynan made it his business to oppose the post-World War II dreariness and austerity and attain a standard of wildness and outrageousness.

He declared himself a "Gangster in the Groves of Academe," a phrase that has a lot of meaning if you consider the things that he dominated. He forced his way at *Isis*, the university literary magazine, and made a reluctant editor give him a post as drama critic. His pieces were so good—which is to say sharp and tightly constructed—that they needed no editing. At *Cherwell*, a fortnightly review, he took a commanding tone and wasn't afraid to say Olivier had "no majesty" in the part of Lear. The tough-guy editor of the magazine, Alan Beesley, was someone Tynan related to—"a tightly packed case of dynamite"—and someone who gave him "a sense of rapport with the Life-Force." Beesley was the enemy of bores and "Group Men," which is to say the hearties and conformists that every college had plenty of. He and Tynan shook things up with a magazine that mixed the scholarly, the edgy, and the pop—articles on Coleridge and Sacher-Masoch and the comedian Sid Field. Ken gave meaning to our expression in-your-face with his cocky, learned, opinionated reviews. He was the same kind of debater, not merely the typical Oxbridge contrarian ready to turn anything upside down, but a personality. When the motion at the Union was "There is No Hope for the Modern Novel" he argued that the motion was about himself—he was "the cheap, flimsy, suggestive" stuff that novels dealt with. Modernism, c'est moi. He didn't mind negative material clinging to his reputation so long as that reputation was growing. And for a second time, in *Cherwell*, he wrote about his fear of insignificance, calling it "the grey evil . . . indifference to being . . . emptiness, sterility." He worried, but with no reason: jealous fellow undergraduates burned his effigy on Guy Fawkes Night.

His dramatic career at the University was anything but gray. Soon after matriculating he joined the Experimental Theatre Club, did well in the part of Iago, and went on to stage and act in numbers of productions. His specialty was the outré: for example *A Toy in the Blood*, his adaptation of *Hamlet* complete with the prince in bed with a prostitute, a gun fired at the audience to signal Polonius's death, a drunken Ophelia calling Hamlet on the phone, and music by Artie Shaw. Some of it sounds like stock-in-trade undergraduate stuff. And some of Ken's posing—the dramatic career of being Ken Tynan—is a bit fey and wearisome ("Neuuurrrotic young men," were his favorite character types). While playing himself—he delighted in his green suit, gold shirts, lavender tie, and much more that sounds like it was left behind from *Brideshead Revisited*—he's often funny and striking, but hard to gauge: is it ironic or serious? Paul Johnson, the prolific historian who was a contemporary at Magdalen, recalled the arrival of Ken at the porter's lodge, complete with luggage: "He turned to one of his bearers and said, 'have a care with that trunk, my man. It is freighted with golden shirts.'" The whole thing even has a touch of Gatsby, which is to say it's an act and a way of life at the same time. It's a blokish dandy playing at being a man of fashion—and for sure it means to assault in a way that no gentleman ever desires. Being Ken is a matter of adapting styles, combining things that don't go together—but being commanding, not laughable. Like John Osborne's idol Max Miller, Tynan meant to captivate, amuse, startle, shock, transgress.

Surely his production of Milton's *Samson Agonistes*, staged at St Mary's, is a gigantic expression of his personal style and all its effrontery. Kathleen Tynan describes it in wonderful detail, and her generalization is on the mark. "Nothing quite like it had been seen before in Oxford, let alone in a church." "Ken found a thirty foot wooden tower used for repairing overhead tram wires, and installed it in the church. He placed his Samson on the top of this edifice—where the audience could barely see him. He had Delilah, her skirts slashed to the waist, wearing gold platform shoes from Portugal, climb precariously rung by rung up the tower." Ken wrote a manifesto about the drama which has some of our blokish themes transferred from the individual to the realm of dramaturgy: a play must generate "attacks," produce an immediate and vital response, shock. "This sad age needs to be dazzled, shaped and spurred by the spectacle of heroism." Tynan, like our other protagonists, wanted to do something that would break away from the "grey evil" of English life.

His romantic activity was also no mean feat. For a while Pauline was still his girl—"Paul," as he addressed her in letters, brought out the tender and poetic side of his nature, his ardor, his enthusiasm for womanly charm, and his outrageousness. On Twelfth Night of 1946 he saluted her with one of his best flights: "I want no more to go a-roving in the light of the lunatic moon." Such a feeling meant that the two lovers should "scoff gently at the idealism, the extremism, the hypocrisy, the shallowness of all we see about us." Again, Tynan is enjoying the spectacle of his own performance, imposing himself, showing off his dizzying rhetorical gifts—Tynan on Mad Love. Never a rough customer in his dealings with girlfriends—nothing like the brusque anti-romantics we have dealt with—he was nevertheless no prize when it came to fidelity. True enough, Pauline admitted to cheating on him once and he flew into a rage. The vehemence of passion was also everywhere in his letters to her. Take this one which the editor dates May/June 1946: "YOU MUST ASSUME (PLEASE) THAT THE ONE INCONTROVERTIBLE FACT OF YOUR EXISTENCE IS THAT I LOVE YOU; IF YOU CAN'T BELIEVE OR WON'T BELIEVE THAT, THEN YOU MUST BE QUITE THROUGH." But then again there's a

letter of May 24—the very next one in the volume of correspon-
dence—to Elizabeth Zaiman, a vivacious chum who worked in
the theater with him and was studying medicine: "I love you
dearly ever dearly. Let that be a lesson to you. An object lesson in
don't-look-so-damn-lovely."

But Elizabeth was not the main medical student girlfriend in
his Oxford days. Gillian Rowe-Dutton, a dark-haired glamorous
heartbreaker at St Anne, caught his eye and got an invitation to
tea. Reflecting on the young extrovert, Jill concluded that he was
"the mostest": "He could switch on intellectual brilliance like a
floodlight." He could also break off his engagement to Pauline,
get engaged to Jill, have it announced in *Isis*, and set up a household with her in record time during the spring of 1947. He was
still a minor and his parents had to sign a document consenting to
the marriage. For a short period they lived expensively and outra-
geously, with Ken supplying the black lace-trimmed camiknickers and a whip. But she wasn't sure of his stability; they spent the
summer in Donegal, not a Tynanesque venue. He was depressed
by the isolation; she soon broke things off. Enter her former lover
on a mission to retrieve the camiknickers. Ken, true to form, went
to the police to complain about their theft.

He supplied another pair—blue crepe de chine trimmed with
ermine—for the next young woman to whom he was engaged, a
philosophy and politics student named Ruth Cropper. And then
he got engaged to another girl named Gillian Staynes, an ethereal
beauty who couldn't take his vanity. It seems he blocked her access
to the mirror when the two were checking themselves out before
entering a dining spot. His antics and transgressiveness continued
with a pal named Eileen Rabinowitz. He wrote her letters about
spanking and his biographer reports that he declared "Sex means
spank and beautiful means bottom and always will."

But being this way was part and parcel of being serious. He
was a student of sensuality and sensuousness—of shapes and
forms and sensations of all kinds. The theater was the best place

for him because it was all about immediacy. But from the start he had been an analytic and descriptive writer, not a creator of original effects. That's not to say he didn't do something major: in fact he made the critic into a literary spokesman for the artist, a philosopher of looking at things. Most theater critics of his time were essentially reviewers: he came forward with many ideas and subjective perspectives for making theater exciting and visceral and dangerous. Straddling the pop and classical worlds, entertainment and Oxford erudition, he became a new kind of critic.

The essence of a Tynan performance was gusto, that quality celebrated by William Hazlitt over a hundred years before. Tynan's essays were filled with energy, physical references, and feelings of delight and vitality. Hazlitt said the artist who has gusto can capture power in nature—like Michelangelo he can "convey an idea of muscular strength, of moral grandeur, and even of intellectual dignity." He spoke of Milton's gusto, which also involved vehemence: "He repeats his blows twice; grapples with and exhausts his subject. His imagination has a double relish of its objects, an inveterate attachment to the things he describes, and to the words describing them." Kathleen Tynan, without mentioning Hazlitt, referred to Ken's gusto in attacking the pop singer Frankie Laine at the Palladium: "he spreads his arms out like a wrestler, and then hits a mad, toneless head-note, holding it so long that you expect him to drop like a stone at the end of it." Gusto is relish, even when the object being described is ridiculed. Here's Tynan on Orson Welles's Othello: the actor is "hunching his blubber shoulders in laughter. The shoulders rise like boiling milk, and he chokes over his own good humour, fuming like an awakened volcano."

The critic who wrote like this was living at a time when gusto was in short supply. There was an energy drain on the stage and in critical discourse. The English theater of the 1940s and early 1950s had a great actor like Olivier, but it had precious little else in the way of "muscular strength." Tynan, the man who feared "grey evil," saw it in the form of the drawing room plays that dominated the West End. His 1954 essay "West-End Apathy," reprinted in *Curtains*, is a hilarious brief account of "the peculiar nullity of our drama's prevalent *genre*, the Loamshire play." It's the "tombstone" of British theater—a kind of drama that recycles the plots of romantic novels and combines them with "the playwright's vision of the leisured life he will lead after the play is a success." "Joys and sorrows are giggles and whimpers: the crash of denunciation dwindles into 'Oh, stuff, Mummy!' and 'Oh, really, Daddy!'" And even solid writers such as Noel Coward and Terence Rattigan are part of the Loamshire slump—the long decline since Bernard Shaw. They don't denounce—they mute the conflict of British life with wit or understatement or good taste. Tynan started to practice his rambunctious critical trade before the British theater had anything out-of-line: he called for gusto and passion when the theater was about refined tempests in teapots.

For all his urbanity and sophistication, Tynan refused to be genteel or to compromise with the genteel. The word gentleman hardly occurs in his writing—in his career it is almost nowhere. A "thrusting man" like his father he never let delicacy get in the way of ambition. Kathleen wrote that after Oxford "he was writing to the drama critics on national newspapers asking for their job." He tried acting and directing, but failed at both. He tried out for a semi-nude review but was considered by the manager of the company to be too queer for the audience—actually too campy, outré, and mannered. Tynan was never involved in the gay life. Another part he played drew the comment from an *Evening Standard* critic that he wouldn't have a chance in a village hall "unless he were related to the vicar." Where he did succeed was in taking that critic's job from him.

Lord Beaverbrook, the *Standard*'s owner, made Ken drama critic in 1951. After having hustled for a living by writing reviews for numbers of fine publications, he was now at the center—only

4 years out of Oxford. Meanwhile he had met and married a rich, magnetic New York Jewish girl named Elaine Dundy. She was literary and ambitious like Ken and would write a best seller about upper bohemia, *The Dud Avocado*. Flashy and in love with the high life, the couple was photographed in matched fake leopard pants, lolling on a leopard sofa.

Ken wrote prodigiously during the early 1950s—about the lackluster English drama, the more exciting American musical stage hits like *South Pacific* and *Top Banana*, and the electric performers, including Alec Guinness, Mary Martin, Ethel Merman. He traveled to New York in 1951 with his new wife, there to meet theater people like Joshua Logan and critic Harold Clurman; in 1953 he went back, took in more shows, and made contact with Cecil Beaton. The old aesthete Beaton and the young critic worked on a literary picture book called *Persona Grata*, a look at celebrities including Garbo and Judy Garland. But fizz and glamour was only part of Tynan's life; he had to work terrifically hard in order to earn as a journalist and he was also on the lookout for more substantial subjects than show biz. When he discovered bull fighting in 1951 he hooked into the kind of performance that suited his serious critical talents. The 1952 season in the theater wasn't much, but the bull ring had greatness on display. Dignity, manliness, courage, "love of grace and valour, poise and pride," "mastery of technique" fascinated and "exhilarated" the young writer.

Bull Fever, published in 1955, was his first book with real staying power: it's a classic about pleasure and danger. It has that peculiar Tynan touch—the marriage of defiant worldliness and learned insight. Our author is immersed in sights and smells, but is always ready to pounce with an idea. Like the toreros he so much admires, he performs with "garbo"—zestful panache. His intention is to lay out the terms of the ring, its rules, and conventions—and then to give accounts of fights in Pamplona, Madrid, and Valencia. Along the way he reports on the charge and risk, the fun, the beauty and ugliness, and the meaning. The book is at once a discourse and visceral experience.

Although he deals in the coolness and discipline of the toreros—and hates sentimentality and purple prose—Tynan admits deep emotion: "I have preferred to be immoderate and go to extremes: I would mistrust any man who could talk about Spain in a monotone." Defining the balance between detachment and feeling Tynan comes up with this: "When the fighter is at his coolest, the emotion is often at its height." Given the challenge of the ring—fear of death, fear of killing a bull in a dishonorable way, fear of indignity—there is also a challenge for the torero and the writer: to keep clear of cheap effects while still being a performer. Tynan hits it nicely, "You don't climb Everest singing hymns."

Yet you must be expressive, find a way to grip the crowd. Tynan does it with his vivid phrasing, a mix of the everyday, the ironic, and the erudite. Of a mediocre torero's performance: "something like hearing one's favorite bits of Pope on the lips of a traffic policeman." His wide-ranging allusions are as precise and exciting as the fighter's cape work. The torero, he tells us, functions like the Anglo-Saxon scop, the public poet entertainer of the mead hall: he must improvise "bizarre and unfamiliar material"—which is to say he must elaborate on the basic story of bull killing. If he disgraces himself by losing "direction" he becomes like the great Litri when Tynan saw him in his period of decline; the critic of the ring beautifully uses Melville to describe "the undraped spectacle of a valour-ruined man." Tynan's commentary is all about risk, threats of disgrace, acts of bold assertion and overcoming—the stuff of aggressive masculinity. Those "cornered giants of tragedy," Prince Hamlet and Hedda Gabler, are both manly and cool as they face desperation and death; they remind him of bullfighters. One swaggerer holding up bull's ears comes to mind: "two ears for Calerito, who strode round the ring like a louche mobster from a film directed by Elia Kazan." And

Charlie Chaplin is a point of reference as Tynan depicts the torero exposing himself "in a spirited, volatile, balletic manner, to all kinds of danger." The little tramp is always at risk, playing with death and delicately picking his way through a menacing world of obstacles. It's not about toughness, but it certainly is about pride and ability to dominate "through the mind rather than the muscles." At a point Tynan turns philosophical as he defines the special coolness and courage of the bullfighter. He uses Lionel Trilling's discussion of Senecan stoicism—apatheia—to sum up his own vision of a brave performance: it's "the principled refusal to experience more emotion than is forced upon one, the rejection of sensibility as a danger to the integrity of the self." This classical courage and disdain for romantic special effects is something that fascinates Tynan: it's a standard for judgmental criticism and living. Tynan's own writing strives for balance—just the right measure of learned reference and personal feeling. Hold the gush and sonorous prose.

That doesn't mean a writer can neglect flavor. Tynan dazzles and amuses with his descriptions of being there. The sensualist enjoys the spectacle of a bad performance: "I whiled away the butchery by accepting too many glasses of sherry from my neighbor, and eating greasy lumps of Pamplona sausage." The Englishman refers to the Fair of San Fermin as "an ordeal by noise and wine." Pamplona is "bull-crazy" and "bull-happy" when Tynan is there. Four amateur bands "play like madmen, each trying to outblow the others." He touches base with all the senses: "The plaza is full to the flag, and reeks of cheap scent and cheap cigars." A train ride after a fight in Segovia is "a riot of harmony, an international congress gone mad with good fellowship." At dinner that night with five strangers he has "gazpacho, the stinging cold soup of the south, metallic Spanish champagne, and paella sticky with lobster and oil."

Noise, smells, tastes, blood, desperation and dignity all in one, Tynan's *Bull Fever* is a remarkable mix. Ultimately it's a sad book because it leaves us with the terrible death of Manuel Rodriguez, a legendary fighter gored by a legendary bull. For Tynan bull-fighting is also about honor and heroism—"the great absentees of western Europe." What greater blow to masculinity could there be than a world without such qualities? Woolly as Tynan's thinking may be—when did honor and heroism finally depart the scene?—it's not so different from Lawrence and Yeats as they attack bleak modernity.

Before John Osborne's great debut in 1956, Ken found most of his excitement in New York, Hollywood, Spain—and the pub-licity arena. He was dissatisfied with the *Evening Standard*—too small a playing field—and only lasted for 15 months; he had writ-ten insultingly about blood-and-thunder old-time star Donald Wolfit and the offended man threatened to sue the paper; the paper fired Ken when he, in turn, threatened to sue it for publish-ing negative material about him. Next he was up to his old game as he succeeded in grabbing Ivor Brown's job on the *Observer*. And he was soon on the move, looking for more than the West End had to offer in the early 1950s. He socialized with James and Paula Mason, the director George Cukor, the abrasive wit and friend of the Gershwins Oscar Levant, Broadway collaborators Betty Comden and Adolf Green. He even lived in Gene Kelly's house for a while, enjoying the sight of Marilyn Monroe making hot dogs. He met Garbo and reported on her screen sensuality: "cupping her man's head in both hands and seeming very nearly to drink from it." He carried on with Carol Saroyan, the play-wright's wife.

When *Look Back in Anger* hit London like the kick of a mule, Tynan was in the mood: "We need plays about cabmen and demi-gods, plays about warriors, politicians, and grocers—I care not so long as Loamshire be invaded and subdued." He explained his critical approach: "I counsel aggression because, as a critic, I had rather be a war correspondent than a necrologist." In an essay in *Curtains* written in 1958 and titled "The Angry Young

Movement" Tynan describes Jimmy Porter as the first character in the modern English theatre who spoke "in our own language, in our own terms." And Tynan anticipated the fuddy-duddy genteel response to "tiresome" angry young men's rhetoric: "the day you stop hearing it will be the day on which art shrugs its shoulders, gives up the ghost, and dies." In his Loamshire essay he had also wittily anticipated the genteel audience's perception of his kind of masterpiece—"a pink-eyed, many muscled, salivating monster."

His business was finding and writing about monsters, developing a critical stance about them, and cutting a figure that met their requirements. Like the critic he most resembles—William Hazlitt—he had to be in touch with the spirit of the age, while also being his own man. After a period in which he had to create his persona against a fairly unhelpful backdrop of Loamshire and Shakespeare, Ken was living in exciting times. When Osborne's *The Entertainer* opened in 1957 he wrote, "For once I felt, mine was an enviable métier." And the mid- and late 1950s were rich years for a theatre man. Osborne wasn't the only outrageous act. There was working-class drama—in working-class language—from Arnold Wesker and Sheilah Delaney; there was Irish hellzapoppin and satire from Brendan Behan; and there was the European experimentalism of Brecht, Beckett, and Ionesco. All of it allowed a critic to fashion an identity, to find who he could be by letting his personality and intellect collide with very good and sometimes great creative works. Ken's gusto could work on more than acting—it had new writing to describe. The interplay of admiration, conviction, and powerful intelligence—and the ever present egoism—made for many reviews that are more than reviews. Tynan believed that writing lived long because of style—and his work gives the belief real weight. He also believed in ideas and a theatre that dealt in intellectual and political conflict. His aesthetic sense was socially charged and unafraid of convictions—even of propaganda.

In *Curtains*, published in 1961, he went to work on the serious business of saying what he wanted from the theatre. We have heard about what he didn't want, but the real excitement comes when he can state his enthusiasms. Stylistically he wanted to get beyond the drawing-room, even beyond the cleverest drawing-room wit. Where are the new English playwrights? Or as Tynan cuttingly puts it, where are the old ones? Well, they're back in the sixteenth and seventeenth century. "High drama presupposes high colloquial speech, which, since Cromwell, has been a rarity on English lips." It's almost as if he's adapting the critical view of critic F. R. Leavis—that English literature has lost the grain and fiber and vitality of its great tradition by becoming abstract and insincere. Restraint, detachment, understatement—even sophistication and discernment—have done damage to the theatre. In the seventeenth century "A stock-pot was bubbling which everyone tasted and tried out in speech; and drama evolved out of an epidemic of logorrhea." This is quite far from witty banter—it's Jimmy Porter's tirades, his raunchy references and riffs and sarcasms.

He called for the visceral, the earthy—and provided the same in his essays. In a review of Vivian Leigh's performance in *Caesar and Cleopatra* he describes the great beauty and wife of Laurence Olivier as "pert, sly and spankable." He's dissatisfied with her work in *Antony and Cleopatra*: "She picks at the part with the daintiness of a debutante called upon to dismember a stag." He loves Ben Jonson's *Bartholomew Fair*: "it has its finger on the pulse, its ear at the keyhole, and its nose in the privy." He's exasperated by moderation, by Gielgud's Macbeth—a performance that fails to horrify. It's as "casual as crochet work" and about as terrifying as "the Cowardly Lion in *The Wizard of Oz*." And he plainly says that he values passion above poetry: the Old Vic *Romeo and Juliet* produced in 1952 gets things right: "you can't rage mellifluously or cry out your eyes in time." He calls for the darting, changeable, unstable beauty of a performance—a Shylock who can move from villainy to "sardonic comedy." English measure is his target: "It needs a Continental actor to switch from fun to ferocity in a split second. Englishmen take at least half a minute to change gear."

This emphasis on passion and energy is also essential for the critic. It's not the yes/no of opinion mongering that matters but the gripping style of the writer. He must find his readers by writing "clearly and gaily and truly" and by regarding himself as a mirror "recording a unique and unrepeatable event." Recording is not simply relating; it must have ideas, attitude, and can even have a measure of propaganda. Teach and delight, Sir Philip Sidney enjoined. Tynan agrees. Demanding an end to convictions and didacticism is like "demanding a certificate of intellectual impotence." Tynan loved Brecht and his bold use of politics and stagecraft—the former are part of what it means to experience the fullness of life. In talking about Arthur Miller he said that theatre is "a dramatic consideration of the way man ought to live." It would seem that the Tynan aesthetic is something like this: the passionate experience excites the critic, runs like a current through his style, and that style transmits felt ideas. These last are not clever situations of the drawing room or leaden abstractions of agit prop. As he says of *Waiting for Godot*, "it pricked and stimulated my own nervous system." He explains that the play made him think of the style of the music hall and the ideas of a parable; but it "banished the sentimentality of the music hall and the parable's fulsome uplift." It offered a "view of life" that couldn't be reduced to entertainment or teaching, but that had something of both.

But for all Tynan's other enthusiasms during the late 1950s, John Osborne was his main man of the theatre, "a lean esurient actor in his twenty-seventh year." Tynan didn't mind the rather tiresome, catch-all label Angry Young Man, created by a publicity man. It was perfect for someone like Osborne, a creative malcontent, an intellectual who disliked intellectuals, "a dandy with

a machine gun." Tynan's celebration of the Osborne manner—
the truculence, the arrogance, the in-your-face way of presenting
class, sex, and suffering—was something personal. He had a lot
invested in this nasty-mannered autodidact. Osborne was his bat-
tering ram in the campaign to knock down the fortress of British
convention. He delighted in his subject's conquests and assaults.
It was wonderful that in 1957 Osborne had a weekly income of
£3,700 when 18 months before he had been an obscure repertory
actor. It was great to hear the British royal family referred to as
"the gold filling in a mouthful of decay." It was also bracing to
watch a man outside the tradition of liberal education and the
university go to work on big ideas, contemporary problems like
Suez and British backwardness. Another Angry Young Man, the
critic and literary scholar Colin Wilson, got savaged by Tynan for
his bestselling book *The Outsider*: here was a case of rebellion that
was mishmash. Wilson intended to introduce the English public
to alienation, Dostoyevsky style, and to champion the insights
of the great misfits in European literature. Tynan found this all
too trendy, irresponsible, and silly. While Osborne had uttered
the genuine cries of the lonely, drifting Brit of twenty-something,
Wilson was pushing a feel-good philosophical position "somewhere between existentialism and Norman Vincent Peale." The
Power of Alienated Thinking. And unlike the restless, position-
less Osborne, Wilson was a believer in the elite of outsiders. So
Tynan's man Osborne stood forth as a rugged, rude, partyless
dramatizer of the contemporary British condition.

But this heroic denouncer of conventional Englishness didn't
have a long run in Tynan's good books. Tynan wanted intelligent
savagery, not just nastiness—and the latter was what Osborne
descended into as the 1960s wore on. While Tynan was ultimately
less toxic than Osborne, both made a fine mess of a once exciting
intellectual relationship. When Tynan's National Theatre passed
on two Osborne plays, the great angry young man fell to abusing
his old defender, calling him a purveyor of "intellectual spivvery."

Tynan had meanwhile been ventilating about Osborne in his journals, writing about meanness, slackness, and the "illiberal self-absorbed, self indulgent" quality of Osborne's 1971 play *West of Suez*. While this material wasn't public knowledge, Osborne was right to detect the unsympathetic, unfriendly side of Ken; his old ally was a detractor. Into this unsavory brew came further squalor as the two of them apparently reconciled their differences one evening in 1974 at a dinner with Kathleen and Osborne's wife Jill Bennett in attendance. Both men could agree on the pleasures of spanking and rolled around in dirty talk while three sheets to the wind. At one point Kathleen refused to add to the merriment by removing her knickers. Osborne took a final dramatic shot at Ken in his play *The End of Me Old Cigar*: a Tynanesque figure is referred to as "a lilac-trousered Oxford trendy with a passion for inflicting 'dangerously painful spanking'." True, enough but not a pally thing to write.

A long time before all this awfulness and acrimony, Tynan's own career and love life became enormously complicated: *The New Yorker* beckoned in 1958 and Tynan entered New York, Kathleen tells us, to take up his post as theater critic like Bolingbroke entering London. During his 2-year stint, he wrote with distinction and lived and socialized at a terrific pace; he came to know Norman Mailer, Lenny Bruce, James Baldwin, Jules Feiffer, George Plimpton, and Martin Luther King. Oh, he also took time out to fly to Havana to see Hemingway who kept a copy of *Bull Fever* at Finca Vigia. At the bar of the Floridita he had many drinks with Tennessee Williams and Papa, and observed the latter's swaggering and bullying. Papa sparred with the lavatory attendant ("When you gonna get old, papa") and was on the verge of gay-bashing in conversation with Williams. He was guarded with young Tynan, a critic who horned in on his bullfighting passions. Not long after this Tynan was in Malaga for the bullfights and Hemingway challenged his authority in matters taurine. Tynan said his authority was his "eyes"; Hemingway said "fuck" them; Tynan stormed out and had the drinks put on his bill. Such was Tynan's power that the next day Hemingway backed off and apologized!

He left *The New Yorker* in 1960 in a blaze of glory. The going away party was at the (enormously pretentious) Forum of the Twelve Caesars and had celebs like Lauren Bacall and Harry Belafonte and literati like Dwight Macdonald. Edmund Wilson didn't show, but wished him well and gave him a rare blessing cum blurb: "the best writing of the kind since George Nathan, if not since Beerbohm and Shaw." The great critic hoped the work would be in book form before long. *Curtains* was soon out—and produced the impact we have described. His next volume—from a writer who was not a book writer—was *Tynan Right and Left*, published in 1967. In it he profiled himself as critic and man and swept through the decade of theater and cinema, also taking a last look at the 1950s and the glory days of Osborne. In summing up Jimmy Porter's ethos, he seemed to sum up his own: "Good taste, reticence and middle class understatement were convicted of hypocrisy and jettisoned on the spot: replacing them John Osborne spoke out in a vein of ebullient, free-wheeling rancor that betokened the arrival of something new in the theatre—a sophisticated, articulate lower class. Most of the critics were offended by Jimmy Porter, but not on account of his anger: a working-class hero is expected to be angry. What nettled them was something quite different: his self-confidence. This was no envious inferior whose insecurity they could pity. Jimmy Porter talked with the wit and self-assurance of a young man who not only knew he was right but had long since mastered the vocabulary wherewith to express his knowledge." In his portrait of himself at the beginning of the book, Tynan can't quite claim to be working class, but he does insist that his readers are "part working class, part intelligentsia." He also embraces Porter/Osborne's idea of love and aggression as inseparable forces: to this vision he links Konrad Lorenz's then famous tract *On Aggression*. In true blokish fashion, he says he hates compromise, but—mind you—not because he's brave or principled. He's a creature driven by work and satisfaction of appetites. He hates metaphysics, codes, rules, but loves people. He loves existing and fears death. "This may account for his instinctive sympathy with the Socialist-maternal ideal of equality and mercy rather than the Conservative-paternal ideals of hierarchy and authority."

This disdain for social and cultural authority is a leitmotif in his criticism. It is best expressed in his review of *Billy Liar*, a play about a working-class young man who likes to float pleasurably in his dreams and fantasies and say to hell with job and responsibility; it goes with saying that Tynan may be throwing out a lot of valuable cultural capital as he takes the side of the undiscriminating and the feckless and the rude: "We have irrevocably (and healthily) renounced the 'gentleman code' that cast its chilling blight on so much twentieth century English drama. No longer are we asked to judge characters by the exquisiteness of their sensibilities, or by the degree to which, in moments of crisis their behaviour is consonant with standards of tact, good form and distinctly muted sentiment." Never mind that Tynan gets gentlemanly behavior—integrity, honor, manners—mixed up with Bloomsbury sensibility, a quite different thing. He seems to have it in for restraint and form and decorum. And that, sad to say, was going to mar the rest of his career after all the discipline and sharpness and perception of his early books. In brilliantly exposing some of the stuffiness and rigidity in theater and life—in appreciating Jimmy Porter with such gusto—he all but paved the way for his own decline; true, he couldn't stand John Osborne at his worst in the late 1960s; but he was a creature of Osbornism—recklessly hedonistic and rather incoherent.

Always louche—and frequently loony—Ken went back to his job at the *Observer* in the early 1960s. His marriage to Elaine Dundy was in tatters, and he soon was passionately in pursuit of young Kathleen Gates, a married lady and a writer who worked in a modest capacity at the paper. Kathleen received a marriage proposal during their first lunch together. Although she took 8 months to fall in love, she did become his most sympathetic and insightful companion. She understood what made him tick—love of the aesthetic moment, passion, flavor, wit. He was on the brink of being appointed as the director of the National Theatre, an honor that carried with it the power to shape a whole segment of the British theatre scene. He was dramaturge, recommending plays, supervising translations, commissioning new work. Laurence Olivier was his boss. Together they wanted a state theatre that was rooted in writers' visions, not commercial schemes and the pursuit of hits. This meant everything from Congreve to Brecht. The great actor found Tynan hard to take, arrogant, full of himself—"too fucking tactless for words." This was the same person who had criticized Olivier in his cheeky review of a *Lear* production back in the 1940s. The young fellow was too used to his own way, didn't know how to go easy. The excessive quality of Tynan the man and critic was his charm, his stock in trade, but also his weak point. Not a bona fide 1960s let-it-hang-out trendy, he was nevertheless out of control in his own way; he insisted on saying fuck on the BBC in 1965. Kathleen, who knew him best, said "he liked to provoke because it was fun."

"I write to become sexually desirable; now that I have what I desire, why write?" Again, provoking and perhaps not quite true. Tynan was a difficult case of blokishness—he liked to celebrate his maleness, his freedom, his aggressiveness. He liked a fight, a spectacle, and was fearless about the mess that ensued. He lavished time and energy—to hell with profit—on projects that anyone canny would have steered clear of. While a player in celebrity culture, he refused to deliver the predictable goods as a writer. When at *Playboy* as a contributor, he didn't quite satisfy— his essays on women's bottoms and undergarments were rejected, too Tynan and specialized for the Hefner publication, too quirky. *Playboy*—when not involved with political think pieces or literary fiction—has tended to be about bimbos, limos, mansions, cash flow, middle-brow philosophizing about sex. Tynan was dangerous, not your writer of businessman-friendly soft core. Blokes from Oxford don't make good playboys; Tynan didn't want to be on the masthead.

But he didn't mind being the prime mover of *Oh! Calcutta!* the sex revue of 1969 that went on to make millions for other people. Tynan wanted to turn his hedonistic ideas into a witty and sophisticated show meant to provoke and arouse. He didn't care about art or social value—the basic value was to be the fun of sex, erotic teasing, and exploitation. He worked hard to get famous contributors like Jules Feiffer and Beckett; he even was worried about the quality—which is to say the coherence and craft—of the skits. He was scared of the law, meanwhile, and signed away his rights to profits. The outcome was tremendous—denunciation in reviews, outrage, the threat of the cops, and a show that would live into the 1980s in New York. When all was said and done, however, the work didn't amount to much for a writer and cultural critic; Ken peddled a skit on underwear and one on sadomasochism, but this is hardly the stuff of literary conquest. Three years of his life went into the show—and New York critic Clive Barnes, a man of discernment, made a fair comment: "I have enormous respect for Ken Tynan, as critic, social observer and man of the theater. But what a nice dirty-minded boy like him is doing in a place like this I fail to understand." The excitement of the revue was rather manufactured, drearily relevant to the age of liberation—beautiful bods in the service of something a bit tedious and heavily tendentious. True Tynan always had a soft spot for powerful propaganda, but then again he warned against being too partisan and obvious. Wasn't he lending himself to something old hat with no clothes on? Something so swinging it would soon be a period piece?

He wanted *Oh! Calcutta!* to be a good dirty show, not a literary work. But in the essay "In Praise of Hard Core," printed in *The Sound of Two Hands Clapping*, he changes his tune about eroticism and art. Lionel Trilling is quoted to support Tynan's seriousness about the marriage of literature and pornography: "I can discover no ground for saying that sexual pleasure should not be among the objects of desire which literature presents to us along with heroism, virtue, peace, death, food, wisdom, God, etc." All well and good—and maybe Tynan even thought that *Calcutta* could meet the standards. But the trouble is that he was so overexcited and taken up with show biz that he said art was crap.

Tynan was in pursuit of raw sensation, sense experiment—and yet he was the literary man with training, standards, fine critical judgement, and erudition. Did the two Kens ever come together? Yes, in the best sensuous writing in *Bull Fever*, in the enthusiasms and visceral responses of some theater essays, and in his accounts of himself and his growth and development. His letters are electric, filled with the charm and excitement of a young man encountering beauty and pleasure. But when he went doctrinaire—or even trendy—he could be awful. No one can lament the fact that he never published his study of Wilhelm Reich. But Ken opining in the papers and magazines, working in the theater, reporting on a bullfight, capturing the aura of a beautiful woman, putting his books together, writing his diaries and letters, discoursing and drinking and smoking a cigarette with his third and fourth fingers—yes. Ken under an orgone blanket is a dark spectacle—no. And it is also disturbing to read of a writer saying he has "outgrown" words and wants to live in a pure world of gesture and sensation.

6

GETTING THEIR OWN BACK

The figures that loom largest in the bloke revolution—Larkin, Amis, Osborne, Tynan—are by no means the whole story. True enough, no others can beat them for sheer talent and ability to throw hedonism and aggression into high relief; yet there are some other writers of the 1950s and 1960s whose signature works made an impact then and continue to be much more than readable today. John Wain's *Hurry on Down* (1953), Thomas Hinde's *Happy as Larry* (1957), Alan Sillitoe's *Saturday Night and Sunday Morning* (1958) and *The Loneliness of the Long Distance Runner* (1959), and John Braine's *Room at the Top* (1957) are imaginative, solidly written books about young men who want something more and something different than the older generation got out of life. These books all deal with defiance of one sort or another, but that doesn't mean they are about proletarian fist shaking and left-wing propaganda. As we have seen, the Brit defiant type needn't be fuelled by a working-class consciousness—he can just as well be a wild, disaffected child from any region of the middle class.

John Wain, a dentist's son who grew up in Stoke-on-Trent, was an only child in a very prosperous household; like Kenneth Tynan's family money, the Wain prosperity didn't go very far back, John's grandfather having been a laborer. The family idea was also like that of the Tynans—to keep one's distance from those humble origins. Wain remembers being warned against the lower classes in Staffordshire, the "rough boys" at his school and in the neighborhood. Unlike Tynan, he didn't make a great splash at his school or have a blazing adolescence; he tried for no scholarships and wound up as a fee payer at one of the less glamorous Oxford colleges—St John's, the college of Larkin and Amis. Humphrey Carpenter's discussion of Wain in *The Angry Young Men: A Literary Comedy of the 1950s* nicely places him in the social scheme of things: not an upper class boy with a sense of entitlement, not a brilliant striver. He quotes from Wain's autobiography to good effect: "I lacked both available kinds of confidence." But Wain did well at the University, loved its beauty, its curriculum, and the dons—and got a First. He studied with C. S. Lewis (Tynan's old tutor), was no rebel, and early on admired Dr. Johnson and other standard authors. He came on just as Philip Larkin was finishing up; nevertheless he caught the aura of intellectual authority and promise that surrounded the future poet. He wanted to know Larkin and succeeded in trailing after him with other "urchins" when Larkin visited for weekends. He went on to start a magazine called *The Mandrake*, publish Kenneth Tynan—not to mention Kingsley Amis's review of Larkin's *A Girl in Winter*. Wain's career had little of the flavor or brilliance of the big legendary men. He was distinguished because of his landmark novel and his book on Dr. Johnson, but he was a tweed-hatted teacher who, after time at Reading University and the BBC, became Professor of Poetry at Oxford, not an outrageous drinker, ladies' man, and self-promoter.

But his blast of resentment against the way things were, *Hurry on Down*, was the first major book of the revolution in sensibility. It came out a year before *Lucky Jim*, and it got a much bigger publisher's advance. Amis was a bit jealous, but in a letter to Larkin he did have to acknowledge that Wain was doing something interesting. He was describing the same "grotesque and twisted view of life" that Amis was trying to capture. Amis then gave Wain a nasty shot by saying *Hurry on Down* was "overwritten," especially in its scenes of people reacting, "slumping and choking and feeling searing pain." This from the man who drew out Jim's final drunk scene, made a book out of Jim's faces and gestures! As it happened, Wain produced a smooth, credible, funny account of a university-educated screw up—something that must have made Amis uneasy. *Lucky Jim* got all the credit and publicity and great reviews, but *Hurry on Down* has a lot to say that's worth remembering, most of it mordant. It's by no means a book that has *Lucky Jim*'s crackle and ingenuity, but it has plenty of edge and is by no means overdone buffo. At the end of the narrative—a drifter's progress downward, socially and ethically—Charles Lumley is not really lucky at all, unless you consider being a cheap radio script writer lucky. True, he gets a high-paid job and a pretty girl like Jim does, but the flavor of the resolution is acrid. Jim got nice things; Lumley got a girl who had previously thrown him over but was now attracted by his media salary.

And yes, Wain was there first. First at expounding bloke philosophy, first at attacking "the artist" and artiness, first to create those scenes of bourgeois and bloke colliding, first to express unromantic lustiness, first to explore that grubby, seedy world that wasn't lowlife but wasn't interested in a better life or a more meaningful life. *Hurry on Down* was involved with the sheer experience of male being, the what-the-hell and go-to-hell of the male psyche. The story begins in Stotwell, a nondescript place in the Midlands picked by Lumley, a recent Oxford graduate. He picked it at random because he intends to live a life at random; he even says his Oxford career was random—"shapeless" cramming— hardly the case in Wain's career. In any event the plot warms up when Lumley hits on the idea of making downward mobility and drifting his object: why not find ways to lose oneself, to shrug off the burden of convention, education, class, others' expectations? For a couple of hundred pages Lumley hurries on down the social ladder—becomes a window washer (no jokes about erotic scenes provided), a transporter of cars, an accessory in a drug ring, a hospital orderly, a chauffeur, a chucker out in a nightclub, a gag writer, and finally a script writer. Along the way he gets a philosophy: "The people he belonged with were ill, disgusting, unsuccessful, comic, but still alive, still generating some kind of human force." Like John Osborne—but years before—he references the "hoarse shouts by red nosed music hall comics" as a way to describe his life. Maybe, like Archie Rice's gags, there's tragedy in the noise, but there's always been some struggle to resist the awfulness around him.

What's so bad about the national scene? About people and customs and manners? Just about everything to drive a fellow to transgress and to worship the "twin deities of his world," alcohol and cigarette smoke. Wain is an expert on nosey landladies, working-class parents filled with pride by a son's success, girlfriends' censorious relatives, patronizing headmasters, dissatisfied bosses. There's Mrs. Smythe who wants to know just what it is her lodger does for a living. Years before Keith Waterhouse created *Billy Liar*, that bloke with the fantastic imagination, Wain had his Charles Lumley telling the woman that he was a Jehovah's Witness, no, actually a private detective. Her rage and tormented syntax deserve quoting: "Just whatever do you mean? And you'd better tell me, young man, you'd better tell me. I've never had any lodger here but what I've known he was respectable, yes, and in a steady job too, and here you come and won't tell me what it is you do and now you come out with all this, a detective, a man that has to mix with criminals, and bringing them to my house before long I shouldn't wonder, that is IF it's true what you're saying."

Wain goes a bit easier on the Hutchinses, a gentle set of working-class parents from up North whom Charles once met at Oxford and encounters by chance on a train. They are in awe of their pompous son George, an Oxford man who made his way, but as Charles remembers, made it by being a sniveling snob

who was too good for his mother and father. This isn't to say that
Charles himself is particularly nice to the older couple; it's their
deference and groveling that drive him crazy.

When Charles visits the Tharkles, the relatives of his old girlfriend Sheila, the awfulness increases. Robert and Edith are incapable of understanding anything that doesn't run according to
type. Charles fits nowhere—not a prosperous business man, not
a workman, not a Chelsea bohemian, and not a tweedy professor. (Without pushing it too far, we might remember that he's a
creature of the age of existentialism, a man who exists but defies
essences and roles.) He also is ungrateful—for what we are not
quite sure. They lay on the guilt—"the smug phrases, the pert
half truths, the bland brutalities." They are dreary Britannia per-
sonified: Robert looks like an Airedale and never slips out to the
pub before lunch, "preferring to open half-pint bottles of gassy
beer which he took solemnly from a mahogany cabinet"; Edith
has a "cackle" and a patronizing I-know-what-you're-up-to manner. Charles, be it said, summons the courage to tell Robert a bit
of what's on his mind: "I was just wondering why no one's ever
found it worth while to cut off that silly moustache of yours and
use it for one of those brushes you see hanging out of windows
next to the waste pipe."

But he's not always this forthright. Even as he desires to hurry
on down—get a menial job, lose his social identity—he hasn't
acquired the "sharp edges" of the ungentle. His manners are generally too good, which is a handicap for the push-and-shove of
real living. When he encounters his old headmaster he's back in
the grip of gentlemanliness. It's true he has summoned up the
courage to apply for a job as a window washer at the old school;
but he hasn't lost his old class sense and his old fears. On entering
the "fake Rugby"—with its store of memories, its shower bath
of Old Boys' "falsity and nostalgia"—he loses his sense of himself. Scrood, the old master, interviews him in his characteristic
way: he peers at Charles as if he were an insect on the wall. This

condescending old fellow, with nothing but lost dreams of a university career still has a strange power over our protagonist. But the rest of the book shows Charles putting up a fight against what he was born to and lived through. Wain has a nice tension set up between the young man's inclinations and his desires: when at Oxford with Veronica, the love interest that he wants to captivate with money, he hears "the sounds of vulgar badinage in a variety of uncouth provincial accents." Those would be coming from new men, types like Larkin's pal Norman Iles. Charles's inclination to be a bit of a snob, to think in terms of boorishness, is what he overcomes as the book goes on. But the whole picture isn't very attractive as Charles adopts a code that has a disturbing core of crudity and me-first assertion. Boors are okay characters.

One of the high points of the book is a section about Charles's romance with Rosa, a decent working-class girl he meets while working as a hospital orderly. His attitude is a strange mix of atavistic snobbery, yearning to break out of that snobbery, and fear of being tied down by allegiance to any definite way of life. He dates Rosa, takes her to the pictures, meets her mum (with the Sunday dress) and dad (with no collar and tie) and family (complete with wise guy Americanized brother), sees the life of humdrum labor and rest and Sunday papers and tea with ham and pickles in the best parlor—and can't quite stand it all. He hears the father's innate dignity of speech—that Edwardian English, the language patterns of the trenches in World War I; but he also hears the "cheap smartness" of the brother's "rapid, slurred" dialect. Looking at the "low brown houses" in the neighborhood, he hears "one of us is your home." It's not a good message—and he eventually flees the entanglement for his next stage of hurrying down. That turns out to be a comic interlude as a chauffeur to a rich convalescent. There he again finds that the definiteness of class and role is life's greatest turnoff. The stifling prosperity and "stage set" of the "spotless" Sussex countryside disturbs him. His employer Mr. Braceweight, a successful business man, is essentially an animated corpse; the man's wife is "entirely without flavour or distinction," impossible to remember when she's out of sight. Braceweight's son, a lout who won't do anything but tinker with cars, is real and alive. He's escaped education, class tastes, parental expectations. "[H]e had cleared at one stride the artificial barriers of environment and upbringing." Wain lets us see Charles's real and painful situation—exasperating and wrongheaded as it is. The national character combined with the class system is not right for the development of the independent male self. But Wain is also shrewd enough to show what the alternative is.

In breaking out of awful respectability and stifling gentility Lumley winds up with a compromise that sounds familiar enough today—he becomes a slickster in the word trade without becoming a creator. *Hurry on Down* isn't some period piece about chaps in old fashioned conflicts. It's about every kind of fraud and duplicity that's still on the market: artists and poets who can't paint and write but can scheme, pseudo-scholars, media chaps who talk hot air. The book shows Charles sighing for freedom but actually embracing every kind of absurd captivity. And it's about coming to grips with the crudely assertive and learning to love it. Charles learns to say "merde" to the pretentious Hutchins when he meets him again as a tutor at Mr. Braceweight's. He learns that it's better to preserve your selfish "neutrality" rather than take a place in the class system with its duties and obligations. He finds that the media world is the best way to be loyal to nothing. But he also winds up writing utter garbage for a radio program, the sort of thing that imitates American shows and is based on the cynical conviction that "The Customer is Always Trite." Where's the male autonomy? Nowhere really, and that's what Wain leaves us with: the bloke's confusion as he makes his best attempt to cut loose.

The collapse of integrity and the struggle to regain it is the theme of another very fine novel of the 1950s, *Happy as Larry* by Thomas Hinde. Hinde is the pseudonym of a baronet and prolific man of letters who wrote books on Capability Brown the landscape architect and other dignified subjects. *Happy as Larry* is not very dignified. The book came out in 1957, a year after *Look Back in Anger*, and it's about a young man who's trying to live vitally in the midst of yet another depressing set of English circumstances—marriage to a girl from a stuffy family, career blues that come from being "a writer chap" in a commercial world, good background but no bright employment prospects, the seedy and sordid world of would-be sculptors, writers and artists, closet lawyers, and old queens. Larry Vincent is also a bit of a rotter—someone who has witnessed his wife being hit by a car near their house and stayed away from the disaster for a whole day. There's a bit of conscience in play, but there's more self-absorption, desire for escape, weariness with responsibility. "I've made a terrible mistake, he thought. I must go back at once before it's too late. He was appalled at what he had done so thoughtlessly without realizing its importance." Larry, like Jimmy Porter and Charles Lumley and Jim Dixon before him, would like to run away from his life. The book opens with a domestic scene—his attractive wife Betty and he are talking about some vague employment prospect for him; they're situated in an untidy flat (with "hire-purchase furniture") rented from a censorious clergyman named Brownlegge and his peevish wife (the latter, like Jimmy Porter's in-laws, looks back nostalgically to the good days in India). Betty is wearing an old pair of trousers and trying to motivate him to get a job. He concludes that it's "a bit late" to learn typing. She thinks she might take in sewing. Instead of ranting like Jimmy or grimacing like Jim or hurrying down like Charles, he does something especially awful when he abandons poor Betty. The remainder of the book is his attempt to give an account of himself—it's really the bloke's apologia, the progress of a dispirited soul who somehow knows that he must get in touch with some vitality, love, and truth.

As the book moves along, Larry the rotter and slacker manages to accomplish something as a human being—he wakes up the reader to the routine hypocrisies of life; he gets back at awful people; and he tries to get beyond his own awfulness to some kind of decency. Thomas Hinde is yet another master anatomist of all the lying, stifling conventionality and hot air that come with being a British bourgeois. The situation is precisely the same as that in *Hurry on Down*: a young man who has abandoned the conventions (or never mastered them in the first place) is faced with people who know only conventions. Larry goes to his in-laws' house in Yorkshire ("'La Recherche' stood alone at the end of a new concrete road") to reclaim his wife and start over. Although he's as drunk as Lucky Jim, he still can see the Prices for what they are. The mother-in-law: "In the early morning her face seemed a little puffy. She was deceptively unformidable. This was her strength. This and her small mind which allowed her to concentrate with so much energy and skill on what she wanted." The father-in-law telling Larry to get out: "He said it viciously spitting out a crumb of toast. He gave an impression of terrible cold anger. His wife inspired him to an exceptional performance. The crumb of toast was a perfect touch." Or take the Sourboyans (Dickens lives in 1957!), a couple who are higher up in society. They're the parents of Evelyn, a young girl who is being courted for respectability's sake by Larry's gay friend Matthew. Mr. Sourboyan's "face was wide, so that its features seemed small and unimportant compared with the great shape on which they were dotted." Amid the sherry and thin soup and pheasant he identifies Larry as "one of these writer chaps." True to his vocation, Larry sees the company clearly: "He watches the forks, gathering food on the plates, rising to the opening mouths, returning empty for more. Up they went . . . at the same moment. . . . It was curiously like the scooping arms of some machine." Larry is also an expert cant detector: it's everywhere. He goes for an interview at the BBC for a position as a writer. A jolly, decent businessman friend has forced his rather nasty wife to recommend Larry to her cousin, a poseur with a polo-necked sweater and unbrushed hair. This fellow hits a live nerve in Larry by speaking of cousin Joan as "one of the kindest people I know."

Larry's reply is a fine piece of bloke candor: "You use simple sincere phrases, but haven't you forgot that liking is an emotion, not discovering good qualities to support an argument? Aren't you destroying feeling by what you say, not respecting it? Joyce isn't kind. We might be talking about different people." Larry's insult is very much in Jimmy Porter's line; it's directed at people who live according to "adopted attitude" rather than feeling.

Borrowed phrases rather than emotions and convictions: the conflict is everywhere in the book. Employers specialize in ready-made responses. Larry gets a lecture about putting your "back" to a job. He has the misfortune to be forced into a situation at the Measurements Office, a place where your job is to go out and check building specifications. There he hears the "dreary generalization about loyalty and trust and doing a good job." Readers of 1950s literature should recall Holden Caulfield's reactions to the prep school teacher who says life is a game and has its rules. Larry in many ways is a grown-up Brit Holden, adrift in a city where everyone lives by his or her platitude, idée fixe, or convention. He's apolitical, years too soon for 1960s protest, non-programmatic, opposed to or out-of-step with everything on offer.

Like Holden, Larry is acutely aware that there's something wrong with him, but he's also sure that the world around him is even worse—phonier, more complacent and stupid, more ugly. At the Measurement's Office he studies his fellow workers and wonders how they could have been transformed from "fairly similar babies into such a variety of grotesques." Were such people happy? Perhaps in a desperate way. Mr. Tweed, who has been 28 years on the job, loves to give uplift speeches at kiddies' birthday parties and Masonic lodges. Other people hide their desperation "behind prosperous faces, behind the hire-purchase walnut suite, the four-seater with mother in the back." The notation here is pure Britain after World War II, with the emphasis on the new possibilities of consumerism. The sarcasm in Larry's voice is rather new. It's a late breaking nastiness directed at ordinary people's material and social aspirations; yet for all the unpleasantness, the voice has a certain cogency. The problem raised concerns British aliveness. Larry philosophizes about the national life—first with a dismal conclusion, then with a flash of excitement: "It was impossible to think that things had once been different. The money had gone on beer, not the hire-purchase, and occasionally one had felt a man." But who feels his masculinity these days? How can such feeling be expressed? Larry looks at the Teddy boys, modish toughs of the 1950s, with a certain yearning: "All the vitality of the young working classes, kept down by malnutrition [during the Depression and the War], now let loose on an astonished country." But he's too old to be a Teddy and too self-conscious and guilt-ridden to go in for violence and transgression. Thomas Hinde's story is about a part-time rebel, someone torn between the exhilaration of selfishness and the call of decency. Proud rottenness is not an option.

A good deal of dithering and vacillating is displayed as Larry can't quite decide how to handle his own flawed character. Betty made him despise himself, true enough, and only by facing his "mistakes" can he "recover." But the problem is still that he had "never agreed to this" reformation. What's a poor conscience-ridden bloke to do? Hinde patches an ending together, a fairly mechanical caving in to decency. It's not up to the standards of the rest of the book.

Alan Sillitoe, the son of a rarely employed laborer from Nottingham, knows his own mind about blokes. He's the creator of two exemplary characters, Arthur Seaton in *Saturday Night and Sunday Morning* and Smith in *The Loneliness of the Long Distance Runner*. Between them, they contain the essentials of bloke life—and they are not worn down by ambivalence or their author's scruples. This isn't to say that they are without complexity and shading; but altogether they are the pure breed—no backing off and regrets for them.

Saturday Night and Sunday Morning was a thunderbolt in British fiction—a very big moment in the representation of the working classes, a sign of the times, a protest novel that had more pleasure and fun than sententiousness. It translated beautifully to the screen, and Albert Finney made its protagonist one of the signature young men of the era. Drinking, fighting, loving, and lashing out in his smoky town, Arthur of the novel and the film has become a powerful icon of the post-war period. Sillitoe was exploring a different region of the new Britannia, not the university-educated lower middle-class boys like Jim Dixon but the sons of the old-time manual workers who were out there in factories themselves. They hadn't moved up in society—and felt not a drop of shame nor any sense of inadequacy. Their story—Arthur's and Smith's—is about a certain kind of pleasure and power; it's by no means the only working-class story in the late 1950s, but it's the most vital and exhilarating.

Sillitoe's own life has been a triumph of getting back at literary and social conventions. Like his fellow Nottinghamian D. H. Lawrence, he is working class to the core of his being, not a creature of the ancient universities, the metropolitan salons, the country houses, the literary magazines. He experienced the brutal and dispiriting side of life—the dole, the terrible poverty of the 1930s, the dim prospects for young men. Bright and curious, he nevertheless failed his eleven plus, closing off that avenue of social mobility, a grammar school education. He quit school at 14, unlike Lawrence who was the product of teacher education. But he shared Lawrence's desire to get abroad. Before realizing his dream, he put in time at a bicycle factory and later at an engineering firm as a lathe operator—the same backbreaking work done by his most famous fictional creation, Arthur Seaton. After serving in the RAF in Malaya during the war, he left his job as a wireless operator and entered civilian life with a pension. He had contracted tuberculosis out East and thereafter had to be hospitalized for a year. This was the beginning of his literary apprenticeship. He read voraciously, everything from the classics to Dostoyevsky. He wrote in imitation of the masters. He became romantically involved with a married American woman Ruth Fainlight while living in Kent; she was a poet and soon they fled the country for France and Spain. (Shades of a greater writer from Nottingham.) In the early 1950s they went to Majorca where Sillitoe made friends with another writer who wanted to say "goodbye to all that," Robert Graves. While an Oxford man and classicist, Graves was also a wild card in twentieth-century letters—not Bloomsbury, not modernist, not proletarian. He liked the young writer and encouraged him to write about his Nottingham and his class. In *Life without Armour*, Sillitoe's memoir, he tells the story of his apprenticeship, a 10-year period in which he wrote constantly and was rejected time after time for work that just seemed out of step with the era. *Saturday* and *Loneliness* both reached editors' desks in the 1950s, but they weren't romantic or modernist or affirmative or idealistic. Sillitoe, possessed of a lot of sense and perseverance and good-humored sanity, simply kept writing and sending out work. He finally succeeded in finding a sympathetic editor at W. H. Allen. The outcome was dramatic—plenty of press, wonderful sales, interviews. His reputation in English letters peaked when he published the *Loneliness of the Long Distance Runner* in 1959. This book was also a palpable hit, earned critical acclaim, and made yet another distinguished film with young Tom Courtenay playing the Borstal boy of the title story. Although he has not been a big literary player since the 1960s, Sillitoe has been much more than a two book wonder. He's a distinguished literary man who wrote many fine stories, a few more solid novels, poetry, and screenplays. He lost his way for a short time in the 1960s due to a silly infatuation with the Soviet Union, but regained it as he got wise to the tyranny of Communism and freed himself from ideology in later books. The memoir expresses disdain for the label "working class writer" and even goes so far as to say that class was never much on the author's mind. While this seems a bit disingenuous, it starts to make sense when you realize that the individual is always the center of things in the work. Groups, social consciousness, movements, partisanship are backdrop rather than focus. The anarchic, the pleasurable, and the transgressive always override the politically disciplined. His convictions come across in his beautifully sustained snarling at class and his deep compassion for his men and women. At his best he expresses himself with directness, perfect mastery of idiom, and memorable phrasing. There is not a clunky naturalistic page in *Saturday* or *Loneliness*.

Arthur Seaton's story is about nothing less than the joy and pain of living. Like streaky bacon, it's pleasure and misery alongside each other. The book is an exacting record of how time goes by for a bloke in Nottingham after the big war. It moves from week to week and month to month. Concentrating on the immediate, it's not much concerned with years. The title says it all. The title also conveys that the book is about getting something for yourself before you pay up. And that's Arthur's main goal—at the tail end of an industrial culture filled with sweat and suffering he wants to locate a good time. Sillitoe doesn't romanticize Arthur's pleasures, doesn't gloss over the disgusting and mindless nature of what it means to have fun. The bloke's life is often gross and stupid. But it's once again—as in *Hurry on Down* and *Happy as Larry*—an attempt to defy what would otherwise be in store for a many a man in modern Britain.

As the book opens Arthur is on his way to the lav at the White Horse Club with "eleven pints of beer and seven small gins playing hide-and-seek inside his stomach." The floors and windows were shaking with singing and noise, and the aspidistra, that symbol of middle-class respectability, "wilted in the fumes of beer and smoke." Arthur falls down the stairs, but don't worry; "the rolling motion was so restful and soporific." He's also not too worried about vomiting twice thereafter, once on the suit of a patron. "Arthur sensed that the crowd was not on his side"; a woman was yelling for an apology. His response is totally without shame: a "strong sense of survival" "impelled" him toward the door and to the house of his married girlfriend Brenda. Swinishness, adultery—who cares? It's Saturday night, "the best and bingiest glad-time of the week, one of the fifty-two holidays in the slow-turning Big Wheel of the year, a violent pre-amble to a prostrate Sabbath."

"I'm worth as much as any other man in the world," Arthur thinks. He knows that he's "soon to be sweating my guts out till next weekend. It's a hard life if you don't weaken." But that doesn't keep him from believing "I'm just too lucky for this world." His animal spirits, his refusal to be ground down by the bosses, his shrewd distrust of people who aren't his sort, his love of sex and fishing and boozing keep him buoyed up. While the middle-class blokes had their doubts about themselves, this man has the most self-esteem we've encountered so far. He "weighed" himself and other people up by a standard altogether different from the middle-class values of knowledge or achievement—not to mention background and education. Basic worth is a matter of some-thing almost inexpressible, a combination of manly aggression, friendliness and pugnacity, a "brutal couldn't-care-less attitude." Metaphorically speaking it was a "black animal stifling the noise of its growls." It commanded respect.

There's also more feeling for women than you might think. Yes, sex and love are rough stuff when it comes to men's plea-sure and right to it, unwanted pregnancies, women's suffering. It should be said that Arthur isn't let off easy when Brenda is trying to induce a miscarriage; he's made to see himself as a care-less louse. But for all that he is no brute. Women were "warm, wonderful creatures that needed and deserved to be looked after, requiring all the attention a man could give, certainly more than the man's work and a man's own pleasure." And Arthur thinks to himself how much pleasure he derives from being nice to a woman. He can't wait to see Brenda. "Serves you right, duck, for being so lush and loving." No true equality of the sexes here, but it's a lot better than Larkin's misogyny, Amis's resentment about paying on dates, Osborne's baiting and berating and trash talk.

Arthur's self respect, love of the pubs, and tender regard for women—despite all the chaos they involve—are only part of his way of life: he also is a professed rebel, a true believer in the class war, an unpatriotic resistor of national causes and wars with foreigners. The real battle is with the powers that be: it's an everyday struggle to maintain the integrity of your pleasure-loving self. As a warm-hearted rebel he doesn't go in for puritanical rhetoric about the illusions of his own class, about old working men who have made their peace with the system. He looks at his father—now happy with his good supply of Woodbines and his telly—and doesn't sneer or mock or suggest that life is made for resentment and protest. Sillitoe was interviewed in the *Guardian* in 2004 and tried to convey his 1950s attitude: when he wrote *Saturday Night and Sunday Morning* he hadn't a thought in his head about being an angry young man. He recalled sitting under an orange tree in Majorca: Jimmy Porter's anger "just didn't mean a thing." Now this shouldn't put us off the task of establishing a connection between blokes. Sillitoe was merely trying to stake his particular claim to representing British rebellion. Osborne and Wain before him had a line—a barrage of rhetoric—that is, in fact, quite different from Sillitoe's attitude: *Look Back in Anger* is tormented; *Saturday Night and Sunday Morning* is bingy. And the Saturday night of wildness is given lengthier treatment than the Sunday morning of complaining.

This said, it's undeniable that Arthur Seaton knows how to rise to heights of anger: although he'd rather have fun, he'll give you an inspired rant every once in a while. In the Sunday morning section he lets loose:

> it's best to be a rebel so as to show 'em it don't pay to try to do you down. Factories and labour exchanges and insurance offices keep us alive and kicking—so they say—but they're

booby traps and will suck you under like sinking-sands if you aren't careful. Factories sweat you to death, labour exchanges talk you to death, insurance and income-tax offices milk money from your wage packets and rob you to death. And if you're still left with a tiny bit of life in your guts after all this boggering about, the army calls you up and you get shot to death.

The wonderful rhythms of this passage are Sillitoe's own—he's turned the subject of misery into a little rhapsody on the theme of being a man. The underlying idea, however, isn't much different from Wain's and Osborne's: preserving that force within oneself. Here it is in succinct form: "To win meant to survive; to survive with some life left in you meant to win." If being alive involves "recklessness" and constant "trouble in store for me every day of my life" (as the final page of the book has it), then so be it. The energy in the last bravura passage, Arthur's farewell to us, comes from facing misery but making it all sound exhilarating. It makes you think that the trouble in life is part and parcel of being a man: "Born drunk and married blind, misbegotten into a strange and crazy world, dragged-up through the dole and into the war with a gas mask on your clock, and the sirens rattling into you every night while you rot with scabies in an air-raid shelter. Slung into khaki at eighteen, and when they let you out, you sweat again in a factory, grabbing for an extra pint, doing women at the weekend and getting to know whose husbands are on the night-shift, working with rotten guts and an aching spine, and nothing for it but money to drag you back there every Monday morning." When he's back there he thinks a lot at his lathe: "violent dialogues flayed themselves to death in his mind." Whatever this may be it's not the dreary, the soporific, the conventional and mechanical existence from which our blokes have fled.

The Loneliness of The Long Distance Runner is about a Borstal boy who wants to get his own back at the governor of the reformatory. He's a talented runner and sure to bring a lot of attention to his prison house. That, perhaps, says a lot. He's sans freedom, pubs, women. The story is about bloke life thinned out to its minimum: defiance and mischief. Smith tells us that he has more "fire and fun" in him than the governor could ever understand. He asserts his human status with wonderful force: "I've got thoughts and secrets and bloody life inside me that he [the governor] doesn't know is there." But the pleasure principle has dropped out of life: Smith is nervous and boyishly resentful rather wildly virile like Seaton. At the center of his life is stewing and brewing. He recalls spoiling the picnic of some posh kids, and this in turn helps him to spoil his own fun: it's a bad memory that becomes his reality. "[A] big boot is always likely to smash any nice picnic I might be barmy and dishonest enough to make for myself." Now Seaton does not think that the good life is barmy; yes, he thinks about "them"—the bosses and the other higher ups—at his lathe but doesn't lose touch with his joyous, anarchic nature. *Loneliness* talks of getting back, refers to fun, but it's enveloped by misery. Sillitoe shows the darker side of bloke life—what happens when anger overwhelms hedonism.

The other stories in the volume are in one way or another bitter rather than bingy. "Uncle Ernest" is about a lonely man who buys treats of food for two pathetic little girls, gets questioned by the police as a pedophile, and finally sinks back into his life of apathy and drink. "Mr. Raynor the Teacher" depicts a girl watcher who has his bit of fun while teaching a class of loutish boys. His classroom has a window that looks out on a shop across the way. Despite passing traffic and other obstructions, he sees girls or parts of girls. The one who most takes is fancy walks out with a young man after work. She winds up murdered. Sillitoe ratchets up the misery as he creates portrait after portrait of suffering adults and children. The bastards—or fate—have done the nasty work of grinding these people down. One or two know how to fight back, but their resistance doesn't count for much. A separated couple in

"The Fishing Boat Picture" represent the general state of human relationships: he would like to give her something, help her cope with poverty and loneliness; she receives his gift, a picture, and pawns it for drink. "Saturday Afternoon," another story of trying and failing, is about a little boy who is left home from a family excursion to the movies and spends time attempting to talk a neighbor out of suicide. "We got pally" says a great deal: both were "feeling black and fed up." The child, however, comes to a recognition about "the coal bag locked inside you": better to live, even if you're "half barmy."

Two of the stories rise above such wisdom. "Noah's Ark" has some of the spirit of *Saturday Night and Sunday Morning*. A group of kids try to bum rides on the carousel at the Nottingham Goose Fair. "The Noah's Ark" is reminiscent of the amusement park scene in D. H. Lawrence's "Tickets, Please"—it's a wonderful escape from everydayness. In Lawrence's story the riders are lovers; in Sillitoe's they're little boys who are very poor and bored. "[W]hen a Noah's ark stood in your path spinning with the battle honours of its more than human speed-power written on the face of each brief-glimpsed wooden animal you had by any means to get yourself on to that platform, money or no money, fear or no fear, and stay there through its violent bucking till it stopped." This is more like the spirit of bloke life than the grim resignation elsewhere in the book. The story concludes with the boys almost getting killed and then walking off with "inexhaustible energy for another year." They go off into the night singing an anti-war song made up by one of their fathers and ending with their own irreverent version of "Rule Britannia": "Rule two tanners / Two tanners make a bob." Our protagonist remembers that he once rode free.

Thrills, kicks, and getting back are also an important element of "The Decline and Fall of Frankie Buller." This tale of Nottingham boyhood is a complex exploration of what it means to be male; it's a recollection of life with the boys, life before one has been altered by education and culture and books and all those things that diminish our feral nature. Sillitoe the narrator sticks close to his own story, offering an introduction in which we see him ensconced in Majorca, with his books and friends and literary life—but also with very distant memories of the person he once was. As he travels back in time he recollects scenes of rough play—stone throwing and "war"—enjoyed with a military leader, a retarded kid named Frankie Buller. The boys from the back to backs in town fought the kids from the housing estates. But this isn't simply a sentimental journey, a nostalgic feel for the old town and its lost ways. Sillitoe "plunged back deep through the years into my natural state." He speaks of books as things one would like to rip out of oneself, "cut them neatly from my jungle-brain." Frankie once let the narrator have a strong taste of animal freedom and aggression. The backward boy wanted to enlist in the army as a Sherwood Forester and his young follower is caught up in the romance of fighting, retaliating (against anything at all), and living in defiance of the local workers and their wives. Nothing as categorizable as a juvenile delinquent, Frankie is a general nuisance and an embarrassment. But in this volume of stories, he and Smith are the most alive creatures. He will be struck down by decent society—given shock treatments to crush his violent nature. But that nature was once something precious to our narrator. Frankie's "coal-forest world"—the world of instinct and play and aggression—is at odds with the "hate and presumption" of the ordinary world. Frankie can't grow up and be awful and rigid and miserable like the other characters in this volume. As the story ends the Sillitoe persona encounters his old companion 10 years down the road. The boy-man is delighted by what he hears about the new film in town, *Saratoga Trunk* with Gary Cooper. The narrator tells him "It's a sort of cowboy picture. There's a terrific train smash at the end." The excitement of Frankie takes us back to the exhilaration of Wordsworth's "The Idiot Boy," a landmark poem about liberated consciousness. There a retarded youngster is depicted as riding at night, flourishing a stick and exulting in his world of pure sensation. Sillitoe uses the romantic moment but pulls back from the joy and release as he shows the narrator in a state of dejection. He knows that "they"—the health professionals and the good citizens—will destroy the "immense subterranean reservoir of his dark inspired mind." But he also knows that he will return to his cultivated adult world minus the magical energy of Frankie.

Sillitoe uses proletarian defiance and randiness, boyish high spirits, even mental backwardness to get across his vision of pleasure snatched from a terrible English world of industrial drudgery. The main thing is to locate your Saturday Night in an awful world of Monday Morning.

John Braine, another man from the provinces, born in Bradford and a keen observer of the business community, works on social materials that are several notches up from Sillitoe's factory life and life on the dole. His *Room at the Top* is about accountants, managers, and owners—a far cry from Arthur Seaton at his lathe. Braine went to St Bede's Grammar School on a scholarship, the typical mark of distinction for a working-class boy who was going places. He was in the Royal Navy, did odd jobs thereafter, and landed in the local library as chief assistant. He tried freelance writing—with spectacular results. *Room at the Top* sold as many copies as the *Odyssey* and *Lady Chatterley's Lover*, which is to say a million. It was serialized in the *Daily Express* and made into a picture starring Laurence Harvey and Simone Signoret. Braine stayed blokish in attitude, eschewing the highbrow and tony: "What I want to do is to drive through Bradford in a Rolls Royce with two naked women on either side of me covered in jewels." Later in life—after never equaling *Room*—he became a truculent Conservative, a denouncer of unions, swinging London, foreign aid as well as a loud supporter of hanging and corporal punishment. (Shades of the two biggest creative figures of the period—Amis, Larkin—and the anti-youth-culture Osborne of later years.)

Braine on the Right and Sillitoe on the Left were very different characters; yet they were both looking for a way out of the dreariness of modern life—the routines that men are locked into if they're not born to privilege. Braine's book is a brilliant study of how to escape and how to regret the terms of your liberation.

Who is Braine's protagonist Joe Lampton? What does he contribute to the bloke ethos? First of all, he's no lasher out against the class system as such. Unlike Wain's Charles or Hinde's Larry he wants to go up to the top; and unlike Arthur Seaton he's not content to rant at "them" and retreat into his hedonistic existence. Joe is from Dufton in Yorkshire; he was born into a working-class family and had the misfortune to be the only young man in town orphaned by a German bomb. Kindly Uncle Dick and Aunt Emily and their unambitious boys ("headed straight for the mills and apparently perfectly happy about it") are his only family. The town has 14 pubs, mills, a chemical factory, a cinema, and a river "thick and yellow as pus." The RAF was a boost of sorts; Joe was in a prison camp where he studied accounting and lived to get back home to a good job at the Town Hall. Not that the position promised much—all around him were the "zombies" of the middle class, the business community's small-time, charmless, unglamorous Yorkshiremen with their blunt ways. The opening of the novel wonderfully depicts Joe's break with Dufton—his arrival at Warley, a better place, a town of some beauty and some good social and economic prospects. "T'Top" is where the best people live in grand Victorian homes; Joe starts by renting a room from Mrs. Thompson not far from there. She's a lovely lady with genteel ways, the right taste in furnishing and teacups, and the self-effacing gentlemanly schoolmaster husband. All a far cry from dreary Dufton, but at the same time an affront to a working-class boy who has no stake in the good life except his talents and ambition. Joe surely can only look on at the likes of Susan Brown, the local young beauty and daughter of a rich owner, and her Cambridge boyfriend Jack Wales, the swaggering son of a car manufacturer. Or can he get a piece of the action? As it turns out—as Joe forces it to turn out—Warley is a town that can be conquered. Starting from his nice new job in the Town Hall he finds his way into good society. Like Dickens's Pip in *Great Expectations*, he hasn't much feeling for his decent Aunt and Uncle back in Dufton, but he isn't quite a heel either. Joe is yet another of our characters who isn't sordid but isn't especially nice or high-minded or self-sacrificing or scrupulous. Watching him fulfill the perfectly understandable terms of his ambition makes the reader uneasy—very much what Dickens's readers must have felt when they saw Pip's snobbery and self-absorption.

Joe, be it said, has no Magwitch to propel him into a better place. This he does all by himself—with a combination of sleazy charm, professional skill, and nerviness. Nothing happens by magic here; it's all plotted out—get the girl, get the clothes and perks. It all takes work and manly drive—two things that Dickens's mover lacked. But the novel does echo the Victorian classic in a number of important ways—Joe falls for a rich girl and his love is tainted by snobbery and a lust for classiness; Joe is more than a little bit cruel; and Joe is made to see himself plain—a climber who broke people's hearts and lived to stew in his own regrets and bad conscience. The voice of the narrator lets us hear Joe's perceptions 10 years later, when he's sick of himself. Dickens did the same thing with the matured Pip. The big difference between the visions of the two works is that *Room at the Top* holds out no possibility of redemption. Joe knows there's nothing to be done, and he knows very well what he has become.

Blokes, as we have argued, are not lowlifes. Joe wants to get away from the early sordid sex life in Dufton and begin on a higher plane. The self-deceptions aside, this is hardly contemptible. He joins the local Thespians on the advice of his landlady and discovers a new life. He sees two things in his new town: a better class of people—and his very romantic-aesthetic class ideal in the person of Susan; a finer and fuller and more real carnality in the person of the unhappy wife, Alice Aisgill. An older woman with a past and plenty of attitude, Alice is married to an ice-cold local business man, a vulgar nouveau riche type whose house out of town looks like "a Piccadilly tart walking the moor in high heels and nylons." He alternates between romancing and eventually seducing young Susan and—with perfect alacrity—bedding the unhappy wife. But the quick seduction is by no means a cheap affair. Braine makes Joe and Alice a Lawrentian pair—loving, rapturously involved with each other's bodies and minds. (Each reader will have to decide if the regional speech the lovers use is over-the-top or sensuous.) A vacation idyll down in Dorset reads like an outtake from a Lawrence novel, complete with wonderful description of the natural setting. It should also be said that these passages make reference to Hardy's Tess, a doomed woman of beauty and passion. This is not the awful stuff of sex in the army or sex as recreation. Joe thinks of women that there is "a physical goodness about them as sacred as milk." He says that "their soft complexities are what give us life." Now of course the problem with all this feeling is that it is eventually conquered by strategy. Joe, a fellow who once could experience strong emotion, has trained himself to become the Successful Zombie, a classier version of the nullities back in Dufton.

A glance at John Osborne's *Look Back*—published a year before *Room*—should remind us that Jimmy Porter was lamenting the same loss—"one ought to care" is Braine's new way of phrasing things. Yet one doesn't—or is Joe's talk about numbness a kind of realization that has moral weight? Joe is a man of some self-awareness, a fellow who sees his own limitations. At one point there's an ironic passage that describes his attraction to the pretensions and gentilities of "Loamshire" theater—the stuff that drove Kenneth Tynan crazy. Poor Joe was once enchanted by the youngest daughter in a play—Susan had the part—who entered with the lines, "Oh hell and death, I'm late! Morning, Mummy pet." Joe found the pseudo-sophistication very "soothing" and enjoyed the trash because the "characters belonged to the income-group which I wanted to belong to."

But despite his self-awareness, he loves the role of aggressor. Dominating Warley, seeing through people, rising above them, getting the best of every situation—in his best grey suit—is his game. He can do it with the cutting remark reserved for the reader. Mrs. Thompson spoke well, and had "no over-buxom vowels of Yorkshire or the plum-in-the-mouth of the Home Counties." Jack Wales, the biggest swell in the book, is four inches taller than Joe, has Cambridge, the "easy and loose clothes," the Aston-Martin— and the girl. In a wonderful passage Joe's complex aggression comes through—he's feeling "absurdly exultant and at the same time envious." What's going on here is that Joe is able to partake of the other man's prestige in a curious way because he intends to "pinch your woman, Wales, and all your money won't stop me." He actually enjoys thinking about Cambridge and the port wine and boating and "leisurely discussion over long tables gleaming with silver and cut glass." It's about power, Jack's power—what Joe is to trespass against in his own way. When warned earlier on that Jack is seven foot, has a beautiful RAF mustache, and bags of money, Joe relies: "I eat those types for breakfast." Is this an echo of Hotspur? For sure it's meant to show delight in himself, an odd and complex thing when you consider that he sees through himself many a time. Joe likes to be called a beautiful brute by Alice—not exactly what adds to Braine's subtlety as a writer. But there are fine sections when the aggressor comes across as totally genuine man, rather than stereotypical hunk. Joe gets young Susan pregnant, and her father—a self-made man with a Yorkshire accent, a factory, and a membership in the Conservative Club—calls the young fellow for a showdown, a mano-a-mano really. Papa Brown tries to buy Joe off, blow him off, but the old bloke is no match for the young one. Summing up his sex and ambition strategy Joe comes up with a wonderfully pithy and expressive statement: "I had to force the town into granting me the ultimate intimacy, the power and privilege and luxury which emanated from T'Top." Critic Leslie Fiedler had this wonderfully trenchant remark to make about Braine: "When he is boorish, rather than well-behaved, rudely angry rather than ironically amused, when he is philistine rather than arty—even when he merely writes badly, one can feel that he is performing a service for literature, liberating it from the tyranny of taste based on a world of wealth and leisure which has become quite unreal."

Although Joe's domination is complete, his disillusionment still gets the better of him. He has achieved his goal by abandoning one point in his program of conquest—Alice. Put plainly, he has abandoned the fullness of life. He has let Brown set the terms of things by referring to Alice as an "old whore" and by succeeding in the strategy of disgusting a young fellow who hasn't a very delicate stomach to begin with. Joe is broken by the revelation that Alice and Jack Wales had a fling. Honor is hardly Joe's thing, yet there's a limit to dishonor, "a sort of Plimsoll line of decency which marks the difference between manhood and swinishness." Yes, Joe has won the game and gotten his own back, but once again—as in many a bloke story—what looks like victory and autonomy is sour and pretty indecent. Alice cracks up in a car after he drops her—and as the last lines of the book have it, nobody blames him.

7

LITERARY LOVE, CIRCA 1960

The signature books by Wain, Hinde, Sillitoe, and Braine are about a rough bunch of men: they will hurt women and even hurt themselves in pursuit of a good time, a goal, or a half-cracked vision of life. Wain's Charles Lumley learns to relish insulting people—and he's the gentlest of the four. Our next question is about the further development of the male personality in the work of the period: what else started to come clear about the nature of blokes in literature during the 1950s? What were they after? Are there any other writers who added to the mix of aggression and pleasure?

Three important books stood at the turn of the decade— each in its own way uncovered a bit of new territory in the male self. They were all about Yorkshire men, but not types who were going to undergo the slickster's progress like Joe Lampton. Keith Waterhouse's *Billy Liar* came out in 1959 and concerns a young fellow who dreams of comedy writing, has three girlfriends, but works as a clerk at an undertaker's establishment. The awfulness of his situation is like that of Dickens's Pip trapped at his bumptious Uncle Pumblechook's seed business. Stan Barstow's *A Kind of Loving* was printed in 1960 and studies a young draftsman who's also stuck in his provincial rut—and what's more, stuck with a very uncomfortable mix of faded romance and vague disappointment about his life chances. David Storey's 1960 novel *This Sporting Life* is the most visceral of the three books, concerning as it does a young footballer's struggle to play, earn, and get some celebrity and love. With plenty of money in his pocket, he nevertheless lives a bit of a dog's life as a boarder with a disturbed widow. Each book reaches for some new insights about British males, especially the ways they learn to make do with their jobs and their women. In an apparently hopeful time—with things looking up in the economy, consumer goods freely available, hardship a distant memory—our writers paint a fairly desperate picture of male destiny. These fellows are apparently in worse shape than John Updike's Rabbit Angstrom in America—it's a hardscrabble existence for him, but his testosterone and rage to live are at a higher level. And ultimately he can run, which is more than a bit of a problem for our men, even though one is a top-rated athlete.

Love is a big problem no matter where you look in these novels—love and lust that is. No sooner do you get it than there are fights, the girl's family, engagement rings, interrogations from your parents, periods of stagnation, her annoying habits, her limitations and yours, your confusions and cruelties. Is there any way back to that "coal forest" maleness yearningly described by Sillitoe? Well, Keith Waterhouse proposed one. *Billy Liar* is about dreaming and fantasizing and riffing on everyday life till you have a fund of power. It's actually the power of self-absorption, a low form of autonomy. This is what the novel deals with—and sucks us into. We certainly side with the screwy, feckless central character in his long adolescent campaign against the dismal people who surround him. A mere 6 years away from *Lucky Jim*, young Billy Fisher has a set of daft defense mechanisms that recall the master; and like Jim, he's hard as nails when it comes to describing fellows and gals. Amis and Waterhouse are up to something similar when it comes to nice and nasty—pushing our face in the difference. Natural satirists, they are both better at the nasty.

What does Waterhouse communicate about awfulness, dullness, vindictiveness, and the whole bag of provincial tricks? And how does Billy meet his world with some real opposition?

The answer to the first question is that he makes Brit dreariness his own by close observation and the verve of his descriptions. By now we're used to the spirit killers, nay sayers, unlovely women and snappish men. But Waterhouse goes about the depictions in his own way—having more fun than any writer but Amis. We're led through a wonderland of awfulness by a boy whose imagination gives color to the objects of contempt and gives life to his own craziness. Osborne, Amis, and Wain went in for the outrageous and grotesque. Waterhouse gets a lot of mileage out of the totally ordinary. Billy waking up in his room and starting the day with family—his head filled with fantasy, the house filled with deadening reality—is an opening almost comparable to Flann O'Brien's opening of *At Swim Two Birds;* a young fellow is possessed by a made-up world but chained to an everyday one. O'Brien's character lives in Irish mythology; Billy in Brit glory—with Churchillian-like scenes of his saving the nation and a band playing "March of the Movies." But the day must start for real—and after he has left his conjured up land of Ambrosia, he faces the music. Mam and dad and gran downstairs are of course old warhorses out of the Dickens collection—their broadly drawn traits and mannerisms repeated for emphasis and with all variations. Mam's signature line: "Your boiled egg's gone cold and I'm not cooking another." Dad's: "I'm not having you gallivanting round at all hours, not at your bloody age." Gran on Billy's dating habits: "He wants to make up his mind who he is *going with.*" Billy lives in a theatrical-filmic haze where he is able to endure domesticity by making daily life into droll drama, turning around his father's enraged lines ("Who are you having gallivanting, then?") and giving dreary Yorkshire the comic class of Loamshire—which is to say turning his family into upper middles in current theatre. Waterhouse has his bloke enjoy the silliness of British 1950s mummy-and-daddy comedies—and also take a jab at his hopelessly out-of-it working-class family. The Loamshire mother is annoyed that Billy is pissed again; the Loamshire father, a company director, will soon have to talk to him about the money end of life. Meanwhile back in the real Fisher household, Billy's mother knows nothing of stage plays but customarily enjoys "Housewives' Choice" on the radio; she's even written to request the playing of "Just a Song at Twilight" and entrusted the letter to Billy. But that is something Billy never had the stomach for. He couldn't send in an illiterate letter.

He writes or tries to write comic bits for performers and has even made contact with a comedian on the telly named Danny Boon. We come to understand that Billy is strictly a pub-gag man with fantasies about a career and romance; he has no scripts. *Billy Liar* is in itself a bloke's progress to nowhere—or put more precisely to where he started. With a wonderful combination of lightness, satiric observation, and feeling for its central character, the story is about a loser who really is dead-on about the losers around him. Waterhouse has let us see that his Billy is cut off from old-fashioned aspirations, conventions—but also charmingly lost. *The New York Times* called Tom Courtenay in the faithful film version a "coltish . . . tagalong" who seemed in the spirit of Godard. The point is well taken because Billy uses his directionless, feckless qualities—plus his ardors—to create a curious assault on good society, logic, and convention. He's really breathless at the end. The young English kid mocking Loamshire while mocking the working class that Loamshire rose above is quite a figure—a man for his season as a social observer, and perhaps for longer. No good identifier of awfulness is ever worth forgetting.

True, Billy cannot write stories and his desk at the undertaker Shadrack and Duxbury has a drawer with pathetic attempts, the odd pages about humorous schoolboys. But the kick is that Waterhouse can use Billy's observations and misadventures to create a top-notch world of British losers. His book is a pungent account of what's wrong and why Billys crop up everywhere.

Waterhouse works in broad strokes but they handle the ideas and feelings of the period very well. Home, work, and romance are his three areas of attention and he catches Billy performing in each. Dad is an autonomy-crusher, an old-fashioned get-a-job snarler who has no sense of what it is to be a lad. Playful and dreamy by nature, Billy's not right for "Geo. Fisher and Son, Haulage and Contractors, Distance No Object." So his father forced him to get a job with the under-taker. The new millennium television character David Fisher on "Six Feet Under" has California funeral arrangements, per-sonal torments, and family turmoils—with plenty of antic and surreal comedy thrown in; back in the 1950s Billy Fisher used to weave through a day at Shadrack and Duxbury in a less com-plex and multifaceted way, but he did live with the hilarity of death—unmailed funeral calendars, wrong brass plates on cof-fins, slickster plans for making caskets more with-it. Home and work were a series of interrogations by parents and superiors, a set of trials that could only be escaped by phantasmagoric out-bursts, nonsense thinking, and (attempted) sex. Again, point-ing toward David Fisher's world: you have to do something to prove you're alive. Billy Fisher makes bad work of it through-out although he shows us just what he's been up against. For one thing it's the age-old British dream of going to London; and like Dickens's Pip, Billy is trapped in his confusion and fears and illusions. He thinks he's a writer of sorts—not the earlier ideal of the gentleman—and doesn't mind impressing girls with his cleverness; he even has a lovely real pal in town named Liz to chat with about London. She's cool, wears a green suede jacket and black skirt and crisp white blouse. She has a bit of that old mocking, challenging quality that reminds one of Dickens's beautiful Estella—she flits in and out of his life, but eventually can't endure his screw-ups and wooly plans. She represents the new, the attractive, the vaguely intellectual, and artistic and adventurous girl.

Meanwhile there are two others, both horrors and both representing nightmarish provinciality. Barbara is a nerd before the term existed, subsisting on conventions and homey truths, constantly eating oranges, and finding every which way to avoid canoodling. She likes to talk about little Barbara and little Billy and the furnishings in the cottage in Devon. And then there is Rita, the blonde waitress from the local coffee bar (a poorly done-over milk bar). She's a toughy who obviously is providing what Barbara has no store of. Not really a character at all in terms of workmanship and nuance—her lines running to the cheapest sarcasms—she is the lower class nightmare that completes the picture of I-can't-take it-anymore.

But Billy has been taking a lot—most of all the compromised way of life he has drifted into. He's engaged to two girls and living two British lives—one delusional, one merely slovenly. Big breaks from reality and silly little departures. Even dizzy Barbara is shocked by his fast and loose dealing with basics. There's nothing in this boy's life to count on, unless you count a mixed up version of the 1940s. Having the rhetoric of Churchill and images from newsreels and films to summon up, Billy is nevertheless bereft. Making hash out of history and memory, he has his father taking part in the destruction of the Graf Spee. In trying to join the high-hearted, he succeeds in being all the more dreary. You might call Billy a bloke who has failed to live intensely enough—no Arthur Seaton.

Out against him is more than a boring family, a dull job, and a weak nature. There is a great deal of cant that passes for courage and tradition and a great deal of junk that passes for innovation. Yorkshire, Waterhouse seems to say, is high on bumptiousness—the bane of the free-spirited bloke. Take old Councillor Duxbury, a local worthy who remembers everything about the town of Stradhoughton and has a "tiresome reputation as a wag." The old fellow is of course Billy's boss at the funeral parlor, but he's a sage and can see into Billy, despite his own self-importance. Billy wants to play along with the old man's "Old Yorkshire" game of how-things-have-changed; he even wants to imitate (falsely) the old man's dialect. In a curiously moving scene that has to do with integrity, Duxbury shrewdly advises Billy to stop playing the fool—"Tha'rt a young man. Tha's got a long way to go. But tha can't do it by thisen." Billy likes to say he doesn't mind dark satanic mills but he can't stand "dark satanic power stations and housing estates and tea shops." Funny and maybe true about the Teddy Boy culture invading the dance halls, shops, and fashions. Things were looking pretty tacky at the X-L Disc B with its "yellow-cone shaped ashtray stands, their bright yellow smudged with black." Superior Billy can go the old man one better in terms of condescending. But let it be admitted that Billy has lapsed into the bumptiousness business himself: "rugged Yorkshire towns, with their rugged neon signs" is funny the first time that you hear it.

Keith Waterhouse had a fabulous run after the appearance of Billy. There were several spins-offs from the first book, some solid work for the London stage such as *Jeffrey Bernard is Unwell* (about a drunken newspaper man), and a long career as a popular newspaper columnist with strong opinions on the integrity of the English language and even stronger ones about people trying to push him around. Some of it sounds like Billy at times: when leaned on by Robert Maxwell, the owner of *The Mail*, Waterhouse said, "I don't work for *The Mail,* the *Mail* works for me. The reply I gave Cap'n Bob." He told Maxwell, "you work for me. You produce the paper in which I write. I am like a music hall act—I am top of the bill at the Palladium." Here Osborne's Archie Rice rides again, with the defiance and the cheerful flight from understatement and common sense.

Looking back on *Billy Liar*, we realize that Waterhouse captures the bluster, the easy cynicism, the noise, the shtick of pub and music hall. But he does not let the negative side of his bloke's existence make us forget a craving for life in the midst of stultifying boredom, a desire for feeling amid droning habit. At hospital with mam—it's the end for gran one night and he has been summoned—Billy hears a strange word that the old woman had been mouthing, a term foreign to their household discourse—love.

The word also has everything and nothing to do with David Storey's *This Sporting Life*, a brutal story of a Yorkshire footballer's rise and early career in yet another dreary town named Primstone. Arthur Machin has a regular job at the big works—run by the same man who owns the local team. But we're made to focus on the sporting life—what can be the bloke's breakout from routine. We begin in medias res with Machin on trial to get a big contract; we watch him grow into a version of American boxer Rocky Graziano, the idol of the kids and the champion who has conquered poverty. We even watch him outmaneuver the money men in getting his first contract. "Big" is always the word that applies to Arthur—except that the whole book is about diminishment in the private realm. "Big" "was no mean elation" and I "could make people realize it." But his landlady is always a haunting presence; Mrs. Hammond, an emotionally disturbed widow with two kids, is always there in the book, refusing to be a warm feminine presence. The narrative concerns the sheer awfulness of romantic frustration and desolation, of having earned no credits in human affection although the crowd on a fall Saturday roars for you.

The way this sporting life divides up is the following: the big pay-off for the owners, the big thrill and the short-term gains for Arthur—and money and gifts for a lackluster landlady, a sorrowful character who has let Arthur stay inexpensively in her back lane house. At first there's no sex with Valerie Hammond—she's too depressed, angry, and shocked by the fate of widowhood—but gradually she lets Arthur become her lover. She goes upstairs with him, accepts treats, big presents, country outings, everything for the children—but accepts with a bad will. Manipulative he is—and knows it. Shrewish and ungiving and unsympathetic she is—and thinks she's in the right. The book's a love and power struggle—with the emphasis on the latter. How much can you do to harm a rough bloke?

Arthur's getting his teeth knocked out at the start of the book is the symbolic action—everything proceeds from the brutality; the plot is about enduring dreadful punishment as a footballer and remaining standing in the Yorkshire struggle for a bit of pleasure and gain. Love, too, is the realm of punishment and Arthur and Valerie go at it in the back lane with no mercy. He won't let her alone: she's an obvious obsessive-compulsive who enjoys suffering and painful memory more than good times. But he's going to use his bigness, popularity, and determination to have his way. He's bargained with the big boys for a good contract, why not bargain for what he wants in romance. But the tack only leads to the worst kind of humiliations—the sneers, indifference, and disaffections that are as painful as bad lovemaking gets.

This Sporting Life tries to pit such nastiness against something that's a bit heroic—low down railing against a decent desire to be big. Arthur is reading *Somebody Up There Likes Me*—no philosophical meditation for sure, but an honest statement of wanting to escape degradation and make your mark. Valerie, meanwhile, wants to say that it's all cheap. He says "people know me . . . Machin's a name that means something in town." Her reaction to triumph and the honest challenge of playing a match is: "You can cheer yourself." The sexual passages are also made disturbing in their grimness and wrenching violence. God knows why Mrs. Hammond's grey wool dress always is the right outfit for going upstairs, but to most blokes it might seem formidable. Arthur fully admits to being disgusted by her tattered underwear. Bedroom language runs to "You're a bleeding man." Aromas remind Arthur of soap powder and damp cloth. Storey is laying on the pain and suffering, even letting one of Mrs. Hammond's children discover them and wonder if they're fighting. What lifts up this horrible scene is Arthur's nature—that of a sexually needy man who just happens to want to love and help the wrong woman. She's right in describing his pride in his accomplishment: "Look at me, keeping a widow and two brats thrown in."

Arthur's proper pride—no simple thing—consists of swagger, apeness, capacity to take punishment, ability to stand for something. He may be tiresome at times—the irony of a crawling champion overdrawn—but he is a vividly rendered man who has missed no pain. His mother and father don't admire him. At the end he's being overshadowed by a new kid on the team. And all along Weaver the owner thought Arthur was an okay player: in a degrading scene he tells Arthur that he doesn't realize all the help he's been given. Arthur's answer is "I felt I deserved it and you don't think I do." That's the bloke credo. The very last line of this book also has the protagonist—like Billy Fisher or Joe Lampton or Arthur Seaton—going on after the psychic and physical beating. Other blokes like Wain's Charles and Hinde's Larry do the same: there are no internal crises and emotional sensations worth mentioning. Suffering is spectacle—the rawness of sport and social aggression—not merely personal hurt.

Stan Barstow's *A Kind of Loving* shows a much less truculent bloke than the fellows we're used to: Vic Brown faces his limitations in a more deliberate and less angry way than the others. In real life Barstow has lived with a matter-of-fact stubbornness that's quite different from the antics we have seen in bloke life. The son of a coal miner, he was born in Horbury, Yorkshire, in 1928; he didn't go far in high school and soon joined an engineering firm in their drawing office. He has spoken about the isolation of the working-class writer of his era—no audience, he claims. Now this is far from the case by the end of the 1950s, yet it does seem to register one man's sense of being alone with his humble themes and people. There's nothing spectacular about his signature protagonist Vic Brown. He loves his family, a pint with his mate, enjoys his fish and chips and good clothes (spurning Teddies and wearers of jeans). His ability to cope with what's facing him—a job with small prospects, a beloved whom he's not sure he loves, a hometown in Yorkshire named Cressley that's drab and unlikely to produce much cash or excitement—shows the bloke at bay: while the others have taken beatings from the class system, their families and communities, their employers—not to mention their own masochistic natures—Vic is ground down by his general attitude. He's probably the most frustrated bloke we've seen, deprived of the big-time rage and resentment of Jimmy or Joe Lampton, not even angry enough at himself as the book ends. He's decided to do his best—an old-fashioned solution to the new, post-war confusion he's in.

That confusion is plainly presented. Vic's a smart young fellow near 21 working for an engineering firm; his taste in music and reading and even in the girl who catches his eye makes him superior to most of the draftsmen at Whittaker's. He spots young Ingrid, not at all a common girl in dress and manner, and they soon go to the pictures, out walking in the park, and to the inevitable lovemaking scenes—one, God help us, in her mother's house. The predictable pregnancy makes all hell break loose— the Browns and the Rothwells are both respectable folk, the former more on the working-class side, the latter more toward the middle. Vic—not in love but deeply guilty—does the very decent thing and does so without rancor or any nastiness directed toward the parents. Yet he's been forced. At work he has come to know a man named Conroy, a rough customer who's so smart and efficient that the bosses tolerate him. Our Vic also learns a lot more. Conroy is a reader of serious literature, has taste and judgment about music—but is not a la-di-da recycler of *Times* and *Guardian* views. And Vic comes to see that there's something fascinating—as opposed to all the drabness around him—about this "short square fingered" creature with the loud mouth. "But I know he's got a good engineering brain and he can turn out a line drawing that's a model for anybody in the office. He's also rowdy and coarse and foul mouthed." The "new slant" is Conroy's: "If you like Dostoyevsky and lousy Beethoven—all right." But don't go "letting everybody know what a fine cultured bod you are." All of which is to say that the Larkin–Amis credo—watch out for those poseurs, name droppers, and fashionable ideas—found its way into the mind of a Yorkshire man who was trying to write about limitations.

Now Vic is by no means a doormat either. While Conroy is railing, he himself has a smoldering anger that erupts every once in a while and actually gives the book its memorable hard edge. "God! I'm glad I'm English." What this means is often not very attractive or decent. Yes, he takes people as they come and is not a violent racist who sneers at the poorly dressed Pakistanis on the scene. But he isn't moderate or easy going if he happens to take a personal dislike to you. Individualism—that great British creed—is his: he doesn't lump people together and prefers to do his hating on a one-to-one basis. When he's at his mother-in-law's in a big scene after a "small crawl" of half of the pubs in the West Riding, he's at his worst; after vomiting on the cream carpet, he bangs on Ingrid's bedroom door, shouting and generally behaving like Lawrence's Morel. It's all so understandable given the mother-in-law's obnoxiousness, but it's all so pathetic. In another scene with Ingrid's loser girlfriend tagging along and making catty and suggestive remarks about Vic, our fellow doesn't laugh off the stuff: "I'll take your pants down and slap your bloody arse" is a bit raw, even for a pest. Yet he's reacting to her "mucky talk" about Vic's legendary love life. He's crude in the interest of combating crudity, a defender of his love for Ingrid and of his own position—both of which are difficult to fathom. It's just the fate of the ordinary fellow who wants and needs and knows right from wrong but sometimes chooses wrong and doesn't know why people won't stop lecturing.

8

The Bloke's Progress

Blokes not unlike Vic have come back these days. After many years of an international counterculture, a powerful feminist presence in literature, and an invasion of new social types in fiction—which is to say after youth and rock and women's issues and multiculturalism—there is a return of the angry male who intends to assert himself, explain himself, and show that he's not simply a hunk of aggression or a minor player. A few writers have carried the torch of maleness, although it's burning in new ways as we move on. Nick Hornby, Martin Amis, A. A. Gill are among the most famous contemporaries who are keeping alive the big themes of bloke life. Are selfishness and aggression interesting anymore? Do blokes have an existential expansiveness that transcends Joe Lampton's pretty crude calculation? Is there anything stifling, class-bound, or routinely boring that's worth putting up a fight against?

Gill is a figure who is less well-known internationally than Amis and Hornby. He shares with those two famous novelists a wonderful gift for insult, invective, and aiming the charges against people who drive a decent bloke crazy. Not that any of them have literary voices that are always decent. Listen to him in *Angry Island*, his explosive book of complaints, and you'll hear all the rhetoric and railing meant to correct Brits—some of it is of dubious worth. Gill's strategy is to survey national characteristics and do this very familiar job in his own as-it-strikes-me way. He's a Scot and as a young person was outside the traditional public school/Oxbridge world. His school was very 1960s with its first names for the teachers and its ragged jeans and Che Guevara posters; his father, however, worked for the BBC. After doing odd jobs and becoming an alcoholic in his teen years, Gill went to work for *The Tatler*, that smartest of papers anatomizing the habits of the smart. *Angry Island* is the result of carefully observing what he perceives to be English awfulness. His task is carried out in a way that connects him with all our figures. The tone and flavor remind one of John Osborne in his memoirs—accentuate the unflattering, the dreary, the cruel, and the nasty. The resentment about the unchangeable cultural habits of his countrymen is like the anger of Sillitoe or the disgust and disillusionment of Larkin. Like Wain and Hinde, he enjoys upsetting the applecart. He has a disdain for the poshness of the South and therefore is an anti-snob like those two Yorkshiremen, Waterhouse and Braine. Although a writer for chic publications, he retails plenty of attitudes chic people don't like—disdain for elegant weekending, contempt for Green Movement sentiment, sneering at mahogany tables that cost a year's wages, annoyance at gadgetry, rage at ancestor worship.

Using the bloke persona to maximum effect, he proceeds to conduct an intricate exploration of what's wrong with his countrymen. He's written a me-versus-them book, trying to be a sensible, reasonably decent bloke facing the barmy and the benighted, and the brutal. If truth be told, Gill is in the howling tradition of Jimmy Porter, except that as an essayist he has to get more specific and try for some reasoned argument. His purpose in *Angry Island* is to discourse on Anglo-aggression in many forms. In the course of doing so, he brings his own temper to a boil and makes us see him as no less menacing than some of the rough types he depicts. He tries to separate himself from the worst stuff in bloke life—soccer hooliganism, national bombast, arrogance, nasty humor—and on the whole he does; but there's still a part of him that's rough and raw and proud of it. He also separates himself from what he believes is the classism and obsession with the past that continues to make the island ridiculous.

There's as much aggression and rudeness in Gill as in those he takes aim at. He accuses his countrymen of being in a perpetual fury and using certain practices—humor, manners, understatement—to cover up their rage. His broad brush history leads him to the following generalization: "the English are essentially an angry people, and that anger has driven them to achievement and greatness in a bewildering pantheon of disciplines." Put another way, Winston Churchill, one of their greatest spokesmen, promoted the fable of "the coming together of the most aggressive and glorious peoples, as if its nation building were divine dog breeding." Gill gets mad at the English whenever they get mad, whenever their blood is up. He enjoys playing the contrarian bloke taking aim at his fellows. He's mad at Charles James Fox, of all great politicians. This fiercely argumentative, witty, high living, deeply humorous and humane man of the Liberal Opposition in the beginning of the nineteenth century is really blokish in the best sense of the word and really no one who should be picked on in our age of doubletalk. He signed the bill to abolish slavery. But this isn't enough for Gill; he's labeled a bully.

Actually *Angry Island* is a rampage through English culture and history. The past is filled with dreadful things—the class system, the dead hand of tradition, and all the arrogance that goes with them; the present is filled with people who can't escape and invent a new nation. (Gill, let it be said, likes Henry Tudor and his son Henry VIII—arguably the two pushiest and most hard to put down monarchs in English history. But later monarchs are depicted as being well-supplied with arrogance and fury without the drive.) The National Portrait Gallery has faces that look with "a quiet aggression, a hooded confidence," a situation that bothers

Gill. Although the Englishmen in the gallery aren't into Italian or Spanish-style grandiosity (the squire and country gentleman setting the tone), Gill scores them for "a show of power, prestige, and bombast." And that kind of awfulness doesn't go away when elaborate waistcoats, velvet breeches, and tricorn hats disappear. Even the trendiest anti-traditionalist Londoners today, even the Goths in their pubs, even what's left of the counterculture is in the grip of English anger, arrogance, and hunger for prestige. As he sweeps through nastiness in comedy clubs, greed in the faux-pastoral life of the Cotswolds, horrible little towns overrun by antique dealers, Received Pronunciation (the bland U-English he himself was taught) and Estuary (the language of the media and cool people), Prince Charles's anti-modernist dream come true—the retro village at Poundbury—it seems like the English temperament is perfectly suited to fights. And Gill's specialty is picking fights with the fighters. He's not even respectful or a bit understanding when he speaks of the old-time hard-drinking Soho journalists who made his profession such a good deal. He insults Prince Charles ("Romance coupled with crass"), which is not a rare accomplishment—his zinger, however, is likely to hurt more than many. Charles's Poundbury would take second place to Olde England in Disneyworld, Florida. He rolls out the bad times, places, and things—in this keeping faith with Kingsley Amis. Admittedly there's something hilarious about his savaging of the artsy/craftsy people in the early twentieth-century Garden Movement: it's like Amis's hatred of anything "different." Gill—emotionally overwrought as he is—wants to fight people who are "embarrassingly barmy." Or in pursuit of their own treasure hoard of relics, curios, and old houses. He hates the National Trust with its the-best-is-all-behind-us message.

This kind of rough handling is both his strength and weakness. He has scored many points against absurdities that pose as assets. And he has shown that many cultural usages—queues, sport, memorials, domestic appointments—are "the safety valves of English anger." Like many of the other blokes we've seen, he's not a lover of Olde England, the hugging of history. (An ancient Cotswold town Stow-on-the Wold—noted for its stone—is "catastrophically ghastly" because of its "steepling piss yellow vanity." Cotwold property today—which many buy and sell quickly, moving to more exciting places—is likened to a passed-around porno magazine.) Savage and bordering on the philistine, Gill nevertheless recovers his balance to remind us of a powerful point: our ancestors achieved great things without nostalgia or worship of the great old days; they had their own force, originality, drive, and adventurousness in looking to the future. Gill sums it up with wonderful succinctness: "Every English generation from Bosworth to the Blitz would have voted unequivocally to go forward trusting in their Englishness, their ability to adapt, to be ruthless, tough and cunning." They didn't hang back with the good taste of the past. This said, Gill doesn't give us much of an idea about what forms are in the making. And yet his own story and attitudes do have value and tell us where the culture might be going—toward a questioning of the bullying spirit. Gill—wild, but self-critical, entertaining but earnest—takes us several steps beyond the ethos of blokes like Braine and Barstow.

Nick Hornby and Martin Amis have tracked the mistakes and excesses of blokes, exposed them more than celebrated them, written cautionary tales about out-of-control men. And yet they both stand up for playfulness and hedonism—the irrepressible desire for sex, freedom and autonomy, a good time, and a chance to break out of new varieties of awfulness. They defend the cause, it should be said, with less vehemence and complaining than their predecessors. Jimmy Porter's rants and mocking of Alison seem as antique as toasting one's sovereign or fainting. And no one could refer to the new protagonists as "very tiresome" young men. We can't quite say of them that there isn't something new, something which reaches into destructive realms only dimly described by predecessors in English literature. In any event, what remains as a constant is keeping up the fight, finding a fight in new times.

Nick Hornby has spoken in an interview in the *Guardian* of his own battle against "a sort of strain of English miserablism." By this he is referring to low spirits, doubts about life's prospects, disaffection with the traditional ideas of school and career success, disgust with the snobbery that was still around. Born to people of working-class origins who moved up through business, Hornby saw his rich father, president of Xerox Rand enjoy fabulous prosperity; he also saw that he and his secretary mother were given the ditch. He did manage to get an English degree from Cambridge, but his response to the studies should make us remember the snarky reactions of Larkin and Amis to their Oxford courses and standard authors. "Studying English was useless, completely useless. It took me years to recover from that. Every time I tried to write it sounded like a bad university essay." The "unquestioning sense of entitlement" among the Cambridge students also did nothing for his spirits. He was not cut out to be one of the cultural elite. His memoir about football mania, *Fever Pitch*, and his book about music, *High Fidelity*, show that he was literary in an altogether tough, populist, direct way. He made it his business to describe what a bloke has to endure and how he has to fight.

That's the focus of *About a Boy*. The book concerns a fellow in his late thirties who has to fight an altogether new kind of battle against convention and dreariness. Once people of spirit battled the strict social system, the depressing culture of poverty, nasty schoolmasters, stultifying Sunday afternoons—and the absence of sex from the face of public life. Now Will Freeman is caught in a very complicated battle to be an idler in a world of busy people. Will is the child of a songwriter, a one-hit wonder who wrote an enormously popular Christmas song. The rest is shopping, television watching, going about London to restaurants and clubs, the drugs and the scotch and the many women. At the end of the century a male is supposed to be acting in a certain way, working, preparing to marry—and having fun on the side. Full-time fun is increasingly suspect—which is to say that the central fantasy of bloke life—having little responsibility and much pleasure—has been damaged. When Will picks up a men's magazine with a "cool" questionnaire, he finds that he rates sub-zero: he's earned the points for clothing purchases, eating in a restaurant that serves polenta with shaved parmesan, taking Ecstasy. But he's earned no points for all the things that most people value—job, family, relationships. Hornby makes him defensive at every turn—those other people are wrecks, ground down by uncool habits, an insufficient play instinct, clinical depression, and a general inability to float and go with the flow of entertainment and stimulation. He's an existential bloke, able to supply his meaning from moment to moment and not at all concerned with what it adds up to. Although he suffers from ennui, he can cope very well, thank you. Vaguely unpleasant in his everyday dealings, he's not the fly-off-the-handle angry young man of another era.

But Will has a lot of things to manage that are peculiar to the new Britain of the Thatcher and Major years. He has a name that suggests the toughness of the Iron Lady and the optimism and determination of Major. Mrs. Thatcher, as is well known, did not believe in "society," an abstraction about economic forces, social tendencies, and us. She believed in individuals and families, going about your business, and not worrying about huge schemes for improving the human race. The same could be said for Will. He hasn't a thought about larger social forces and conditions—about poverty and plenty, corrupt public life and greed, the everyday injustices that impact on a nation (for instance, the people who might be living in the next flat). He doesn't believe in such things. Once had an idea to work in a soup kitchen, but dropped it. Ironically (and nastily) used a single parents' group to find women. Really, what do people want from him? He's got his own business to attend to.

Keeping the world at a distance—not doing too many favors, not being people's godfathers, not getting involved generally—is this bloke's enterprise: we've seen it before in Larkin's life and poetry, in various cool scenes in Amis when characters take the selfish way out. In Will's case, married people's lives—with the complications of children, clutter, and general lack of smoothness—are unenviable, although obligatory if you want to be of your time. Bonds and relationships and closeness are in—and Will doesn't have any desire to be part of all that. The book is about how he changes and becomes a reformed bloke. It's basically about how he recognizes that there is a society, not just a collection of selfish individuals.

Will has to work hard to be idle, rather mean, and careless. It's not easy to fill the hours of the day with pleasure and avoid giving anything much to those around you. Hornby does his best to make pleasure seem robotic, grim, but necessary. Our bloke is out every night, but it's not the old matey thing at the local; as a matter of fact, there are no mates featured. That once beery world of camaraderie is now replaced by sleek restaurants. Togetherness, Christmas, group outings with kiddies are all rather disgusting. He might as well be a Scrooge for the new age. He's planning to take drugs and watch videos on Christmas Day. Which is to say that the pursuit of pleasure and the flight from "them" has become a desperate cultural position—it's hard to sustain. Will's Cratchit family, as it were, is a collection of oddballs. There's 10-year-old Marcus, a maladjusted, uncool schoolboy marooned with his emotionally disturbed hippy mother Fiona; there's his pot-smoking dad (not on the scene); there's his (you wish) girlfriend, a teenager from hell who befriends him. Outside this mix there's Rachel—a cultured, beautiful, creative woman whom Will falls for. But what would she want with a bloke who doesn't do anything or care anything about anything?

It turns out that Will possesses a kind of toughness that makes him an effectual man. It's the ability to fight British everydayness—to say no to all the predictable yeses of his world. Rachel thinks he's "tough" in his head, which is to say mentally resilient.

He's been able to resist romantic dreams (like Marcus's mother's hippy world and the counterculture), day-to-day career building and householding, and the hard core desperation that might come from neglecting those two options. He just goes from one thing to the next: exercising, episodes of TV programs, Nirvana albums. And he doesn't have a big philosophy: it's really the bloke holding himself together and holding himself apart from those who would bend him or break him. Put unattractively, it's Will the fashionable bloke about town, "with the cool and powerful, and against the alienated and weak." Put in Rachel's terms, it's a kind of triumph over nothingness that one can't help but admire.

What Will passes on to young Marcus—because this is with all its quirks, an initiation story—is the set of skills necessary to be a modern bloke: how to defend yourself against smothering and bullying. Marcus develops a "skin" and becomes "as robust and unremarkable as every other twelve-year-old kid." After hanging out with Will—much against the cool man's desire—the boy puts wimpiness and singing Joni Mitchell songs with your eyes closed behind him. It's all about toughening up in New Britannia for Marcus; but for Will it's about gentling—learning to love Rachel. Once said however, this doesn't mean a bloke is not a bloke—a man won't give up on his special, aggressive way of enduring.

And now for the bottom of the barrel—what the bloke became when he was more out of control than the out-of-control Will Freeman. Martin Amis actually wrote the worst case scenario a dozen years before Nick Hornby: it's about John Self—no secret in the significance of the name—and how he ruins himself in the world that Hornby's character also knows—consumerism, recreational sex, media obsession, and too much money. Amis's man is, let it be said, a far more dissolute, aggressive, and dislikable character than Will. And in a larger perspective, the strong, coarse fiber of the bloke as we have known him is replaced by the disgusting, disintegrating self. In the course of the narrative, Self jets between London and New York, trying to direct his first feature film. Fully employed, it's true. But his version of bloke life is so supercharged, swollen, and gross, that it's only fair to ask some first-order questions about him and the world he (well) wallows in. It's also fair enough to wonder what has happened to our innocent blokes of the Sillitoe generation with their pub pals, their ventilating, and their usual fun with the girls. Where has the borderline decency of the bloke—one's own pleasure with a measure of sense—gone?

Amis is the man to tell you. What *Money*—his brilliant account of bingeing, drinking, screwing, spending and wasting—tells us is that life is filled with pain, indecency, betrayal, and everything that the blokes of yore fought against. Amis studies a degenerated social type, someone who has lost his autonomy because of the market forces of the media business. This is just the sort of defeat that humiliates the true spirit of the bloke. John Self, if truth be told, is not his own person for most of the book. He lives in the grip of an outrageous new film project, its colossal expenses, its clownishly stupid and egotistical actors, its speed and absurdity, its incoherence, and double dealing. He also is possessed by his personal problems, acquired as a maker of short films and commercials—porno, alcohol and pill addiction, gross ignorance (almost total abstinence from books), gluttony, and a tendency to punch out his doxies now and then. Amis is in the great tradition of gross out—disgusting the reader with human swinishness in the manner of Henry Miller, Céline, Joseph Heller. He has fun with vileness, with lowlife characters, and with all the dishonesty that comes with the territory.

For all this, John is still given a conscience of sorts. He won't have relations with a pregnant prostitute; he can't forget what good is—even though he chooses bad ninety percent of the time. Raised in Pimlico and Trenton (his mother was American), he's known the rougher side of life forever. As a boy he learned street fighting and the finer points of head butting. Success in commercials—an ad for Hamlette, a pork roll, that features a girl in bra and pants cheering up the Prince—has brought lots of money and a chance for tons more. *Money* opens in New York, with Self swigging a bottle of duty-free, fighting with a cabbie, and soon thereafter meeting a sleazy collection of business partners. Amis gives us a muscular/macho send-up of Kirk Douglas in Lorne Guyland; this phenomenon of the screen is famous for having played just about every commanding character in history—including Ghengis Khan and Michelangelo—and for being a champion athlete and major player with the chicks. The leading lady in the picture is no lady, but a recruit from the porn world. Self gladly partakes of her favors. He also seems to welcome the sex shops of the West Forties, the massage parlors of Third Avenue, and the know-how of his steady but tricky girlfriend Selina. Described variously as a golddigger pushing thirty, "an exhausted sack artist with shrink-ing assets," a combination of the "primly juvenile and the grossly provocative," pornography's best competition, she is also strictly "High Street" in tastes and therefore just right for our coarse bloke. It's anyone's guess how much of this is satire directed at the behavior of late twentieth century bad girls or just plain rambunc-tious, raunchy prose for the hell of it. Amis makes things ugly at times, but he also makes them hilarious. Take John's descrip-tion of Selina and her like: "Modern sack-artists aren't languid Creoles who loll around the boudoir eating chocolates all day, licking their lips and purring, their whiskers flecked with come and cream." No, it's all about business, efficiency and money.

John depicts a "new crop of space invaders" who are "plunder-ing the West": "Every time the quid gets gangbanged on the inter-national exchange, all the Arab chicks get a new fur coat." The money men rule "with their wads, the crap they talk, their cruel, roasted faces. I am one." He and his pals from his old ad agency invade a London restaurant at one point. They throw bread, spray champagne from bottles, do dog imitations on the floor, sniff a girl's stockings. A conservative couple watch, "retract slightly and lower their heads over their food." John's crowd end with a few choruses of "We are the Champions." And they are. They have money; excluded almost forever from good company, from the society of the educated and well-bred, they are getting back. "You try getting us out."

Now Amis elaborately prepares Self's downfall. He even has Self aware of the fact that his "private culture" of awfulness is something to escape from. The trouble is that the only thing real at the end of the book is John's acknowledgement of defeat. True, he has a loveable down market girl named Georgina (no sleek beauty), but otherwise no resources whatsoever, no cashmere coat, no nothing. And, sadly, there's the admission that he'd leave Georgina for Nina or Lina or Tina if he had money. Our deflated bloke seems to have lost any power of resistance.

Such a funny but dark account of bloke life was written by a second generation bloke—an aggressive, hard-edged teller of his own truths who doesn't often calculate consequences. Like his father Kingsley he has put in serious time as an insult monger and purveyor of offensiveness. But that's only part of what makes him a phenomenon of bloke life with something new to say. If John Self goes down in defeat, Martin Amis himself has shown a few ways to endure. His memoir *Experience* is rich in feelings that go far to make him a better sort of bloke. In critiquing his father, himself, and many friends and relatives, fellow authors, and intellectuals, he gets a chance to show what he admires and will stand up for. His aggression is different from dad's in the sense that he's able to see beyond it, understand how it gives fire to life but also threatens to destroy life. Now when it comes to shaping a plot, creating believable characters, and putting together a world of wit and manners, Martin Amis has yet to measure up to his father; his seriousness about politics and history, the big themes he has taken on, still have not produced a fictional character to equal Jim Dixon. But the son has humanized bloke life in *Experience*, offering something better than his father's *Memoirs*: while those had a good deal of score settling and snarkiness—not to mention uneven writing—Martin's *Experience* combines the pugnacious and the compassionate, weaving together manliness and tender feeling. His memoir describes how a bloke is both toughened and torn apart in a lifetime. You get to see how one bloke loves and can't stand another, how Martin endures and joyously celebrates his father. Any look back at Kingsley's account of his father is likely to result in the same verdict: mean-spiritedness. *Experience* is not pervaded by that, and, be it said, Martin and his brother and sister were put through the full range of Amis's sarcastic wit, awfulness, drunkenness, incoherence, and adulterous conduct. That's what *Experience* is essentially about: watching a bloke in full.

Martin catches the spectacle of Kingsley, often three sheets to the wind, delivering pronouncements on everything from service in restaurants to English usage to Nelson Mandela's politics. The "ruggedness of his heresies," namely his insulting ways of referring to women and minorities, was something that Martin took on with relish and wit. Nothing better than giving it to dad about his social views. But sometimes things got very serious indeed, and Martin has a moving way of depicting the worst—Kingsley came over one Sunday for lunch, noticed Primo Levi's *If This is a Man*, and commented "What's that you're reading? Some Jew." Martin then recounted to his father an incident about a detention camp in which the Jews were selected for Auschwitz. A moment later Kingsley broke down completely and said: "That's one thing I feel more and more as I get older. Let's *not* round up the women and children. Let's not go over the hill and fuck up the people in the next town along. Let's not do any of that ever again." It took a lot of courage on Martin's part to reveal his father's casual anti-Semitism; it also took a lot of decency and honesty to recognize the old man's sorrow and feelings of remorse. Kingsley is a horror and a human being within the course of a dozen lines.

On the whole the book shows Martin becoming his own man as his father had become his. He's too cool and knowing to lead us through his father's life and point out the faults. It's more a matter of dramatic scenes showing Kingsley as the gifted, fabulously successful writer who was still a waster of sorts. Yes, Kingsley had the drive and ambition to produce a prodigious number of excellent books. He was the child raised in the shadow of Chapel, as he once said, and was no idler. And yes his hard work and jollity ("the duty to be cheerful," as Martin puts it) and honesty and freedom from cant inspired and touched those around him. But in another sense he got stuck in his retrograde politics, his sexism, his arrogance, and his bottle. The scenes of a writer talking about language and craft are far outnumbered by the spectacles of Kingsley falling down drunk or shooting his mouth off or being selfish (not above trying to grab a peach away from a child). Martin at one point breaks out and tells us what's wrong with his father: in a contrast of Saul Bellow and Amis, we hear that the former deals with the "permanent soul," the latter with "the firmly social, quotidian and end-stopped." Yes, Jim Dixon is no Augie Marsh, no delver but that of course is the whole point of Kingsley and of many another bloke. They find satisfaction in the beautiful surface of the world and frustration in every form of ugliness and rigidity. Martin has a metaphysical turn of mind, a daunting list of profound subjects that inform his books, and a tendency to expand the bloke's world. Why must a fellow confine himself to Kingsley's novel of no manners, books about people struggling (often in a nasty way) with sex, their own egos, and society? For Martin things have become bigger—which is not to say artistically more satisfactory.

John Self is a bigger hedonist than any of Kingsley's men—he's also, at times, a slob. John Self—for all his disdain for books—thinks at a higher plane of abstraction than Jim or the others. He thinks about how money and desire and status work globally, how he has an ironic part in a scheme to take away his money. He's the director of a film that isn't going to be produced because the producers have concocted a scheme to fleece John. Martin works on a larger canvas than dad and the bloke has acquired a capacity for philosophical questioning that goes well beyond the angry young men's questionings. The trouble here is that an increase in sophistication, an infusion of philosophical conceptions of the self, all the trappings of postmodern life, do nothing to impress the selfhood of a character on the reader. John Self's hundreds of fast-food meals and Scotches and masturbatory sessions and beddings and cash outlays and impressions of girls—all lovingly described—are rather weightless when put on the scales with Jim Dixon's hilarious lecture on Merrie England. Self is about loss of self; Jim is about ourselves, about men of some understanding and spirit up against the timeless suspects—the inept boss, his favorites, the whole degrading system.

At this late date something must be said about the enemies of bloke life, those who are angry about all the fun and sensuality and rough play and social criticism that make up the bloke heritage and the bloke revolution. One of the best of them has located the bottom of the barrel, but failed, I believe, to trace it to the right literary sources. Theodore Dalrymple, a former psychiatrist and these days a practicing essayist, has taken on the problems of coarseness, crudity, and brutality and made it his business to track the deterioration of our culture—from where he sits. Dalrymple is an angry Englishman himself, scarred by a hypocritical Communist father who raked in the profits as a businessman while spewing the party line and keeping his copies of Lenin and the others at the ready. Dalrymple's mother had escaped Nazi Germany and come to England where she worked hard as a firewarden during World War II. The child saw devotion to an ideological cause and devotion to an open society in his own home. He chose the second, but there's plenty on hand in modern Britain besides the remnants of Stalinism to disturb him. The immediate—and most nauseating—forms of national degeneration can be seen in what many Britishers consider entertaining. This is the subject of "What's Wrong with Twinkling Buttocks," an essay published in *City Journal* in 2003 and reprinted in *Our*

Culture, What's Left of It. Dalrymple discusses two contemporary British figures, singer Marilyn Manson and artist Glen Duncan. The *Observer* had given them big play—and Dalrymple wants to give them the kind of jeering and savage criticism that Gill gave his foes. Manson's act consists of grossing out his audience and making it all seem like ironic, postmodern play. He trades in fun with the deaf (covering them with raw meat), retailing incidents of "smoking exhumed bones for kicks," and using his own act as a Nazi rally. The *Observer* critic found the transgression the mark of "an artist." Glen Duncan's art show, DARK, SATANIC THRILLS, is heavy on sado-masochism—and has also won praise. With this stuff at the ready, Dalrymple proceeds to look for the cultural origins—and you may have guessed that *Lady Chatterley's Lover* is the usual suspect. The 1960 obscenity trial is Dalrymple's defining moment in the moral history of the next half century. The beginning of the end for public decency. A bloke who was interested in sexual warmth has to take the rap for cold exploiters. An artist who wrote beautifully about nature, family life, social class, transcendental yearning, working-class resentment is written off as Dalrymple takes a line at random—about Connie's twinkling buttocks—and proceeds to trash Lawrence as artist and thinker. In the last part of the essay Manson and Duncan are called Lawrence's "progeny." I'd say if you want to know the real culprits, try the crowd depicted by Martin Amis in *Money*: they're really not interested in coarseness at all; it's all about titillation and slime and cash flow.

Dalrymple's other concern that impinges on bloke life is the matter of fighting for maturity in a culture that favors adolescence. He has denounced the coolness that has spread everywhere, the frustrated rage directed against the art, literature, and conventions of the past. By another name this is part of the culture wars; it includes Britain's half-century battle between blokish expansiveness and gentlemanly discipline. Our blokes wanted to shake their fists at the old order—at Bloomsbury and the official literary culture and the gentility that came with them—but they were not perfectly successful in throwing off the past. Individual writers, cultural figures, and cultural productions are never quite bloke or gent; it's a matter of tendency. John Osborne dressed like a country squire, but was saturated in the culture of the music hall; Kingsley Amis held the English poetic tradition in his head, but scoffed at a lot of it; Philip Larkin believed in decency and social piety, but was often harsh and painful to know and anything but a gentleman. Our men were on the bloke side of things, but that doesn't mean they didn't imbibe various amounts of tradition. The figures we have considered were never really a school or a movement. Instead they were stormy or joyous or gloomy witnesses to what was wrong with their elders and juniors—and many of their contemporaries. They wanted a way out of modernism—the dominant tendency of their young manhoods—and they used a style that was older, more rooted in the satire and rhetoric of pre-twentieth-century literature. So what happened? They became retro for the multiculturalists and feminists and experimentalists of the late part of the century and the new millennium. They became the old order. Their successors like Martin Amis and Nick Hornby have of late given the bloke a new life. The master theme continues to be the fight.

Author's Note

An interpretive and historical study like *Blokes* inevitably rests on works that have preceded it. It is my pleasure to notice the most important of my sources here. The social and political story of Britain after World War II is well and clearly told by Alfred F. Havighurst, *Britain in Transition: The Twentieth Century*. Fourth Edition. (Chicago and London: The University of Chicago Press, 1985). Corelli Barnett's *The Lost Victory* (London: Pan Books, 2001), is essential for grasping large economic forces that affected people's daily lives and attitudes. David Kynaston's *Austerity Britain 1945–1951* (New York: Walker and Company, 2008) is a fine, detailed history of the period. Richard Hoggart's *The Uses of Literacy: Changing Patterns in English Mass Culture* (London: Chatto and Windus, Ltd., 1957) is still a classic work for an understanding of non-genteel taste and opinion in the twentieth century. Arthur Marwick's *Culture in Britain Since 1945* (Oxford: Basil Blackwell Ltd., 1991) is a compact and useful summary of highlights.

Malcolm Bradbury's *No, Not Bloomsbury* (New York: Columbia University Press, 1988) is the most incisive, informed, and entertaining account available of what happened in Britain after literary Modernism. The essay that gives the book its title is an analytic piece about the novels of Kingsley Amis; "Closing Time in the Gardens," about the writers of the 1940s, surveys the period and its characteristics. The primary sources cited in "The Bloke: A Very Short Literary History"—works from Chaucer to Orwell—can be found in many editions. I found Christopher Hitchens's *Why Orwell Matters* (New York: Basic Books, 2002) pungent and to the point about Orwell's Englishness. Peter Mandler's *The English National Character: The History of an Idea from Edmund Burke to Tony Blair* (New Haven: Yale University Press, 2006), is rich in detail about the middle of the twentieth century, the hostility to the gentleman, and the image of the "little man"—with his cheek and charm—during World War II. *The English Gentleman: Images and Ideals in Literature and Society* (New York: Ungar, 1987) by me, surveys the styles of life and behavior patterns that the bloke rebelled against. Harvey C. Mansfield's *Manliness* (New Haven: Yale University Press, 2006) is a searching, brilliant treatment of what's right and wrong in the male power drive.

My account of Larkin's life and times employs the monumental research of Andrew Motion in *Philip Larkin: A Writer's Life* (New York: Farrar, Straus and Giroux, 1993). Facts and quotations from the early years, the Oxford days, the career as a librarian and poet are gratefully acknowledged; interpretations—unless attributed to others—are mine. See also Christopher Carduff's penetrating article on "Larkinism" in *The New Criterion*, September 1993. Individual poems considered come from Philip Larkin, *Collected Poems*. Edited with an introduction by Anthony Thwaite (New York: Farrar, Straus and Giroux, 2004). *Jill* (London: Faber, 1964) and *A Girl in Winter* (London: Faber, 1947), Larkin's novels, do not exhibit his aggressive side, but they are nevertheless important for a full understanding of his personality.

Any critic of Kingsley Amis's work, any analyst of his character and persona, must be deeply indebted to Zachary Leader for his exciting, well-written, and balanced biography, *The Life of Kingsley Amis* (London: Jonathan Cape, 2006). I have used the book for details and general background, but have carefully considered as well Amis's *Memoirs* (New York: Summit Books, 1991), a matter-of-fact, rather dry account of his early life and the friends of later years. Leader is the place for the outrageous stories about drinking and womanizing. In any event Amis said that we would find his nature in his books, a piece of advice I have taken to heart in my rendering. The ones discussed here are *Lucky Jim* (London: Victor Gollancz, 1954), *That Uncertain Feeling* (London: Victor Gollancz, 1955), *I Like It Here* (London: Victor Gollancz, 1958), *Take a Girl Like You* (London: Victor Gollancz, 1960), and *One Fat Englishman* (London: Victor Gollancz, 1963).

Osborne's two volumes of memoirs are a major contribution to English literature and literary culture, and I relied on them heavily: *A Better Class of Person* (London: Faber and Faber, 1981) and *Almost a Gentleman* (London: Faber and Faber, 1991). They tell a familiar story of growing up poor and achieving extraordinary success and they do so with rich period detail from mid-century Britain, sharp social commentary, and self-scrutiny. My chapter also owes a great deal to John Heilpern's exciting, empathetic, yet truthful biography, *John Osborne: The Many Lives of the Angry Young Man* (London: Knopf, 2006). Heilpern's treatment of Osborne and his affinities with Tennessee Williams is excellent. "Damn You, England" is an Osborne broadside, particularly violent in tone, directed to his "Countrymen" and published in the form of a letter to *The Tribune*, 18 August 1961. It rages against nuclear armament, the Berlin Crisis, and brinksmanship. The plays considered in this volume are *Three Plays: Looks Back in Anger, The Entertainer, Epitaph for George Dillon* (New York: Criterion, 1958), *Luther* (New York: Criterion Books, 1962), and *Inadmissible Evidence* (New York: Grove Press, 1965).

Kathleen Tynan's biography *The Life of Kenneth Tynan* (New York: William Morrow and Company, Inc, 1987) is excellent and, together with the volume she edited, Kenneth Tynan Letters (New York: Random House, 1998), it has provided me with the full story of youth and Oxford and starting out; *The Diaries of Kenneth Tynan*, Edited by John Lahr (New York: Bloomsbury, 2001) also proved illuminating. For Tynan's major criticism and reporting I have relied upon *He That Plays the King* (London: Longmans,

Green, 1950), *Bull Fever* (London: Longmans, Green, 1955), *Curtains* (London: Longman's, Green, 1961), *Tynan Right and Left* (New York: Atheneum, 1967), and *The Sound of Two Hands Clapping* (London: Jonathan Cape, 1975).

In my chapter entitled "Getting Their Own Back," the novels I have considered are John Wain's *Hurry on Down* (New York: Viking, 1953), Thomas Hinde's *Happy as Larry* (London: Mac Gibbon and Kee, 1957), Alan Sillitoe's *Saturday Night and Sunday Morning* (New York: Knopf, 1958), Alan Sillitoe's *The Loneliness of the Long Distance Runner* (London: Allen, 1959), and John Braine's *Room at the Top* (London: Eyre and Spottiswoode, 1957). For good social background and biographical detail on Wain and Braine, especially, see Humphrey Carpenter, *The Angry Young Men: A Literary Comedy of the 1950s* (London: Allen Lane/The Penguin Press, 2002). Sillitoe's autobiography, *Life Without Armour* (London: Robson Books, c. 2004) is a well-told story about Nottingham poverty and the difficult ascent of a young writer without education.

Finally, works cited in "Literary Love, Circa 1960" are Keith Waterhouse, *Billy Liar* (New York: W.W. Norton and Co., Inc, 1960), David Storey, *This Sporting Life* (London: Longmans, 1960), Stan Barstow, *A Kind of Loving* (New York: Avon Books, 1960), and those cited in "The Bloke's Progress" are A. A. Gill, *Angry Island: Hunting The English* (New York: Simon and Schuster, 2005), Nick Hornby, *About a Boy* (New York: Riverhead, 1998), Martin Amis, *Money* (New York: Penguin Books, 1986), *Experience* (New York: Vintage International, 2000), and Theodore Dalrymple *Our Culture, What's Left of It* (Chicago: Ivan R. Dee, 2005).

New York, 2008

INDEX

Larkin, Philip (*continued*)
  147, 152, 169, 171, 175,
  177, 186
All What Jazz 31
"An Arundel Tomb," 46, 47
"Annus Mirabilis," 46
"At Grass," 47
"Aubade," 40
"Church Going," 39, 41
"Dockery and Son," 32
"Essential Beauty," 41–3
Girl in Winter, A 38, 133
"Going, Going," 41, 42
"Here," 41
"High Windows," 40, 42
High Windows 48
"I Remember, I Remember," 26, 41
Jill 23, 38
Less Deceived, The 38
"Mr. Bleaney," 40
"Money," 46
North Ship 138
"Old Fools, The," 50
"Party Politics," 38
"Self's the Man," 50
"Show Saturday," 47, 48
"Sunny Penstatyn," 41, 42
"Symphony in White
  Major," 26
"This Be the Verse," 50
"Titch Thomas," 43
"Toads," 44
"Toads Revisited," 44, 45
"Vers de Société," 49
Whitsun Weddings 48
Lawrence, D. H. 2, 16, 19, 21, 26,
  27, 31, 33, 34, 59, 121, 143,
  150, 155, 169
"Horse Dealer's Daughter,
  The" 19
"Jimmy and the Desperate
  Woman," 19

Lady Chatterley's Lover 20
Sons and Lovers 17, 33
"Tickets, Please," 19, 50
"You Touched Me," 18
Leader, Zachary 54, 56, 64,
  78, 118
Leigh, Vivian 101, 123
Levant, Oscar 121
Lewis, C. S. 30, 111, 133
Lloyd, Marie 84
Logan, Joshua 118
Lorenz, Konrad 127
  On Aggression 127
Lowell, Robert 25
Lorre, Peter 109

McCarthy, Joseph 68, 93
Macdonald, Dwight 127
Magdalen, Oxford 63, 110, 113
Mailer, Norman 126
Major, John 176
Manchild 6, 7
Mandler, Peter 6
Mandrake, The 63, 133
Mansfield, Harvey 53, 58, 97
Marlborough College 57
Martin, Mary 118
Maschler, Tom 6
Mason, James and Pamela 121
Maugham, W. Somerset 5
Melville, Herman 119
Merman, Ethel 118
Metro-Goldwyn-Mayer 30
Michelangelo 116, 180
Miller, Arthur 124
Miller, Henry 23, 179
Miller, Max 81, 91, 101, 113
Miller, The 89
Milton, John 22, 26, 59, 111, 113,
  116
  Samson Agonistes 113
Monroe, Marilyn 101, 121